Praise for *Press Releases*

"If you're new to PR or not getting the results you want out of your company's PR program, this book is your roadmap to understand how editors think and how to make your efforts more successful."
—Doug Chapin, President and CEO, GlobalSight

"As a CEO, I thought I had a unique PR strategy…First, send a press release every week to show progress. Second, to be picked up by the Tier 1 publication is only a matter of a phone call, right? Third, EVERYONE loves to read my press releases, heck, they would pay to read them if they could…Every chapter in Linda's book predicted my 'unique' strategy and explained why it isn't so."
—Ori Eisen, CEO, The 41st Parameter

"A definite must read for executives challenged by today's world of consumer generated content. Linda's 'to-the-point' approach cuts to the core, using great examples that demonstrate how effective PR is a continuous process, not something you turn off and on when you think you'll need it."
—Rod Lenniger, Executive Vice President, iCrossing

"As someone who has been in the public relations trenches for more than two decades, I found Linda VandeVrede's book an easy-to-read, yet comprehensive treatise on the do's and don'ts of an increasingly complicated craft. I wouldn't hesitate to recommend it as 'must' reading for any corporate executive or public relations practitioner."
—Steve Cody, Managing Partner & Co-Founder,
 Peppercom, Inc.

"As a syndicated columnist who receives PR materials daily, it is my wish that every PR person would read… no, not just read, but study… no, memorize…. VandeVrede's new book. She understands what it takes to transform a publicity person from a nuisance to a welcomed and respected ally."
—Dale Dauten, King Features columnist,
 "The Corporate Curmudgeon and Kate & Dale Talk Jobs"
 and author of *The Gifted Boss*.

"[The book] is a compilation of good points and information for newcomers to the field as well as senior executives."
   —Andy Marken, Marken Communications,
      for *Public Relations Quarterly*

"What VandeVrede has done is put all the best PR advice you've ever tried to give a CEO into one handy little book. And—ever thinking of the target audience—VandeVrede has managed to do it in a book that can be read in a two-hour plane ride."
   —Katie Delahaye Paine, Editor/Publisher,
      The Measurement Standard

"…a nice introduction to public relations for an executive at a small or midsize company…I especially liked the inclusion of ethics and legal regulations, which are so important in this day and age." .
   —Stephanie Houser, President, Launch,
      for *The Phoenix Business Journal*

"Bullseye! With 25 chapters of practical tips and techniques for developing and driving public relations programs, VandeVrede takes a fresh look at the reasons why so many companies fail in their efforts."
   —Sarah Bannan, Assistant Editor, bizAZ Magazine

"I use this book in my public relations campaigns class to give students an introduction to what they will encounter in the working world and how to 'hit the ground running' in their first public relations job. VandeVrede truly drives home the idea that it isn't any one element, but a total comprehensive strategy, that will make a public relations plan successful."
   —Joette Rockow, Lecturer,
      University of Wisconsin-Milwaukee

"One of the best lessons in this book is that the editor is your boss. Not the product, not the company. The best thing that a PR rep can do for me is enable me to deliver something relevant, honest and timely to my readers, not waste my time whining about how I covered the competition at the expense of covering their client."
   —Lisa Vaas, Associate Editor, *eWEEK.com*

PRESS RELEASES ARE NOT A PR STRATEGY

AN EXECUTIVE'S GUIDE TO PUBLIC RELATIONS

Linda B. VandeVrede

SECOND EDITION
Foreword by Dan Miklovic

First paperback edition published 2005.

Cover design: Bill Greaves
Cover illustration: Getty Images
Photo: Brian Fiske Photography
Interior design/layout: The Printed Page
Editing: Claire Gerus
Printed in the U.S.A. by www.booksjustbooks.com

To order this title, please visit www.vandevrede-pr.com or call 480-551-1258.

VandeVrede Public Relations, LLC
www.vandevrede-pr.com

ISBN 13: 978-09762527-1-9
ISBN 10: 0 9762527-1-6

Library of Congress Control Number: 2006908974

All product and service names mentioned are the trademarks of their respective companies.

Disclaimer

This book is provided as an educational guide for its readers. Use of or reliance upon the information set forth in these pages shall be at the user's own risk and shall not establish any contractual or other legal relationship between the author and the users of this information.

Contents

To Dale

Acknowledgments

It's doubtful any author can claim to have finished a book without the support and expertise of a surrounding brain trust of experts and friends to guide the project from concept to completion. This author is no different.

After more than twenty years in public relations, I have been fortunate to meet, work with, and correspond with a host of talented people in their fields. I am honored that so many have agreed to provide their wisdom and insight in the introductory quotes and comments for each chapter. A few brave souls read through the early manuscript and provided helpful comments to make it as useful a guide as possible.

To that end, thank you Dan Miklovic, Paul Gillin, Amy Roach Partridge, Keith Larson, Lynne Habenicht, Tom Blondi, Francine Hardaway, Kevin Parker, Gene Wang, Andy Chatha, Cushing Anderson, Tony Bracanovich, Frances Emerson, Frank Benassi, Roy Heffley, Tony Friscia, Mark Wheeler, David Greenfield, Michael Saucier, Julie McCollum, Kevin McHolland, Tim Moman, Dale Vecchio, Rozanne Bonavito, Steven Weinberg, Juan de Leon, Erik Lien, Tom Inglesby, Marla Hoza, Garth Andrews, Bill Hankes, Kelly Wanlass, Doug Chapin, Derrick Bell, Lisa Vaas, Michael Lasky, Steve Smith, Bob Parsons, Linda Welter Cohen, Dale Dauten, Susan Fallon, David McCann, Heidi Brashear, Nicole Yox, Anthony Helmstetter, and Steve Cody.

I'm grateful to Sue MacDonald and Katie Paine for their substantial contributions to the chapters on blogs and measurement, respectively.

Thanks to firms iMemories, TeleDirect and Transpara for permission to include some of their PR samples in Appendix C of this guide.

I also owe thanks to several experts in the publishing industry for their assistance with the second edition, including Pam Swartz, Karla Olson, Claire Gerus, and Lisa Liddy.

There remains one last yet critical factor in the successful completion of this project, and that is my husband Dale. His constant encouragement and support enabled me to translate my years of expostulations about PR to printed form.

Foreword

As an industry analyst covering software for over ten years I have received literally thousands of press releases. Fewer than 1% of these had truly useful information in them. Companies today are wasting millions of dollars on ineffective communications. Linda's book will help any company trying to gain more from their PR dollar. The clear, concise information, presented in an easy-to-read, easy-to-understand style, is essential to any company engaged in PR.

The audience for PR material is broad and diverse. If you limit yourself to using press releases to get a three-line mention in the back section of the average industry trade journal you are missing the boat. Yet, through ineffective PR strategies, that is exactly what most companies achieve with their PR efforts. This book helps you understand who the audience for your PR efforts should be, how to entice them into wanting more, and most important, how to build interest and excitement in what you, as a company, are doing.

Press Releases Are Not a PR Strategy captures the essence of what is wrong with so many entrepreneurial companies' marketing efforts today. They focus on blasting out PR pieces in hopes of getting mentioned in a magazine to gain credibility. Even larger companies are not immune to falling into the trap of using press releases in a shotgun approach to gaining coverage. Targeted public relations activities can help the start-up achieve market recognition or reinforce the leading image of an industry stalwart when done well. Done poorly it is simply a waste of time and money.

Every single chapter will provide valuable insight to the new PR person, as well as the seasoned marketing veteran. Take the lessons to heart. Learn from Linda's years of experience and you will discover that PR can bring your company impressive returns for your investment.

Dan Miklovic
Managing Vice President
Gartner, Inc.

Dan Miklovic is a Managing Vice President at Gartner, Inc. and has been involved in sales and marketing of technology for over 20 years.

Introduction:

What PR Can Do for You

Have you ever wondered why some companies receive a lot of PR coverage? Do you have an image of what kind of PR you'd like, but just can't seem to get there? Do you become frustrated when seeing competitors with inferior products and services beat you to the punch with feature articles in the key trade magazines?

Whether you are a corporate executive, a PR professional, or a student learning the ropes, you have the ability to apply basic principles to your PR programs that will increase your effectiveness. It is not "black magic" where you say a few words and hope your audience behaves the way you want it to, nor is it a circus ring where you can hawk your services.

PR has become an increasingly difficult discipline. As we move deeper into the 21st century, both the environment for public relations and the people practicing it have changed. Fewer of those responsible for PR have been formally trained in it for any length of time. The prevalence of the Internet has made dissemination easier—both a boon and a thorn to those handling damage control. The old model of mass-to-mass communication has evolved to include new models of self-selected, one-to-one communication in the form of blogs and RSS feeds. Legal regulations such as Sarbanes-Oxley carry tremendous importance for those practicing PR, regardless of whether their companies are publicly or privately held.

Today, editors change jobs far more frequently, making it a challenge to forge lasting relationships with the media. They are also bombarded with a huge volume of announcements via email hourly, daily and weekly. As a result, many have retreated even further behind their virtual walls, becoming more impervious to companies' attempts to promote their products.

Consequently, the challenge of implementing successful PR programs has never been more difficult. But while the times have changed, the nuts and bolts that have always been behind successful PR still exist. Unfortunately, today's executives either never knew the basics, or are too impatient to practice them.

In the following pages, I share proven approaches to making sure your company's innate strengths are made known to the right media. And most important, they are steps that do not involve spin, manipulation, or questionable and unethical practices.

The chapters are organized to take you from a basic understanding of public relations. I'll explain how it differs from marketing communications tactics that directly target the consumer, then describe how to create the necessary materials to implement programs that show results. You'll find a new chapter on emerging media, including blogs, podcasts, wikis and RSS feeds. There are also several sections on specific PR tactics, and how and where they should be used.

Don't forget to check out the PRSA code of ethics in the Appendix—these principles should guide your communications activities.

The philosophy behind successful PR is simple: the **editor** is your main client. Your primary client is not the company, the product, your boss or your sales team. These are important, but if you use them as your primary motivator, you will fail.

What do I mean by that? Keep your focus on the goal of identifying the subject matter in your company's day to day operations that is *most* relevant to your target editor's needs. Then, provide the information in a form and substance that is preferred by him or her. Stop viewing PR as a "free" conduit to promote your company directly to customers. If you can get your head around this mindset, you will see results. Intrigued? Read on.

Linda VandeVrede
Scottsdale, Arizona

Chapter 1:

What is PR?

———

*"PR-savvy companies build mutually beneficial relation-
ships with journalists and opinion leaders and use trust and
support to help media people meet their goals. While there are
never any guarantees that PR will pay off, it can be the most
cost-effective use of a business' marketing dollars. Great companies almost invariably have great PR organizations."*
 —Paul Gillin, Principal, Paul Gillin Communications

———

For the purpose of this book, public relations, or PR, is
defined as that component of marketing communications whose
target audience is primarily editors/reporters, and whose purpose is
to paint an accurate picture of a client's strengths and differentiators.

One of the noted textbooks on public relations by Cutlip,
Center and Broom defines PR as "the management function that
establishes and maintains mutually beneficial relationships between
an organization and the publics on whom its success or failure
depends."

Public relations is not the same as publicity, which is primarily one way (sender to receiver) and geared towards a large mass

audience; nor is it clever manipulation of public opinions and views, known as "spinning." It is also distinctly separate from other marketing communications tactics that target the buyer directly, such as brochures, advertising, direct mail, and special events.

In contrast, public relations targets the **influencers** of buyers, and therefore has much less control over its results and output than do the other, more direct forms of marketing communications. PR is often the most effective route for communication strategies, however, since the information is often filtered by editors before reaching the masses, thereby adding significantly to its credibility.

It's important to point out that PR is not sales support, either. Unfortunately, this is the misconception of many executives who oversee both the sales and marketing functions. Under this approach, marketing and by consequence, PR, are subjugated to the reactive nature and goals of sales. When PR is used as a method to drive sales, the focus shifts from the more productive "What information does the editor need?" approach to "What can I cram into this self-congratulatory press release that will get customers to buy?"

This unconscious shift is probably the single biggest contributor to the failure of public relations, and the reason why marketing and sales should be led by two separate individuals. Public relations should be used to educate, not to sell.

At the opposite extreme, another common misconception is that PR can be conducted independently of other marketing functions in order to save money, and can be turned on and off at will, much like a faucet. To be effective, however, PR takes its cues from the company's overall marketing plan, which sets the strategy and messages for the company. Without a marketing plan in place first, and without the added reinforcements of integrated, synchronized marketing communications, pursuing PR is a waste of time and money.

Examples of public relations deliverables include press releases, corporate backgrounders, editor-focused webcasts, feature articles, books, white papers, and speaking opportunities. The goal of PR is to intelligently and ethically raise awareness within the media. In contrast, examples of customer-focused marketing communications deliverables include advertisements, brochures, data sheets, direct mail, e-blasts, trade shows, and user conferences. The primary goal of these events and tactics is to generate leads for sales.

Chapter 2:

Top 10 Misconceptions About PR: Do They Apply to You?

―――――

"If there is one mantra that public relations folks should take to heart, it's 'know your audience.' It makes an editor's blood boil to continuously receive press releases on subjects that have no place in the editorial context of his or her magazine."
—Amy Roach Partridge, Assistant Managing Editor, *Inbound Logistics* magazine

―――――

The following represent comments heard over the years from bosses, clients, and prospects. If you have ever uttered or believed any of these claims, then this guide will help you better understand what PR is and does. It will also show you how to recalibrate your PR efforts for increased awareness and revenue.

1. **Sending press releases out every 2–3 weeks is a good public relations strategy.** (Not really—you're just jamming the industry with releases that won't be read! Unlike newsletters, press releases should not be issued on a preconceived,

regular basis, but rather, when the news, strategies, or material events justify it).

2. **If I write the press release with jazzy copy, it will get the editors' attention.** (Press releases should be written as straightforward documents that might potentially become legal "evidence" in a subsequent merger or acquisition, not as brochures).

3. **PR should be used to support sales**. (PR's role is to support marketing, not sales—marketing is more strategic and long-term).

4. **PR should be our primary marketing tool because it's free**. (PR is actually not free, and is best employed as part of an integrated marketing communications campaign).

5. **If we really push the edge with our PR, we'll get the editors' attention**. (The only thing you'll push are their buttons, which isn't a good thing! Editors do not respond well to PR that is pushy or pesky).

6. **Our new product will be ready next week, so it's time to put together a press release**. (You're late! The time to plan PR for a product launch is several months before the product is GA— Generally Available. This allows you time to solicit the valuable input of analysts and other third-parties who can provide insight regarding the optimum tone, timing, slant, scope and content of the launch).

7. **The analyst (or editor) who doesn't understand our product is an idiot.** (The fault of the miscommunication is the person who threw the ball, not the one who dropped it. If an analyst in your industry doesn't understand your product, you're not explaining it well and need to reconsider your PR approach).

8. **We should promote David to handle our PR for us—he's young, energetic, and really knows how to aggressively promote the company.** (Hire someone in PR who has experience. Don't degrade the profession by assuming that anyone can move into it. The more aggressive one's personality, the greater chance that he/she will inadvertently turn off the editors with a naïve "kitten with new claws" approach. Even more dangerous, he/she is likely not to be aware of the legal ramifications of PR and get the company into trouble).

9. **If we see an industry issue bubble up, we need to hop on the bandwagon and get our message out there fast.** (Unfortunately, by the time the industry controversy is hot, you've lost your window of opportunity—like the famous hockey player Wayne Gretzky, you should skate to where the puck is *going* to be).

10. **Our competitor's press release contained a complete lie, so we need to be fast in the market and come back with a strong counter-attack.** (Never use press releases to wage competitive war; focus on your company's strengths rather than countering what the competition is doing).

Over the years, I've heard some reactive, kneejerk comments from executives who viewed PR as a controlling mechanism rather than as two-way, interactive communication. I was working for a large multinational company when we invited a key editor to the headquarters to hear about a new product we were launching. Instead of querying us about the product when he arrived, however, the editor seemed more concerned with digging up rumors that we were to be acquired. After the visit, the marketing executive called me sternly into his office and admonished me with, "Your job is to manage the press." As a PR professional, however, your job is not to "manage" the editors and analysts—they are doing just fine. Your job is to ensure they receive the correct information. You cannot control what they think or do. (Note: the multinational company was never acquired, and the product received positive coverage).

Chapter 3:

First Things First:
The Editor is Your Client

"The most effective public relations spring from long-term, ongoing relationships in which the editor can come to rely on your PR representative as a responsive resource. Wrangle a customer quote in time for a tight deadline, round up a non-commercial backgrounder that builds the case for your company's expertise, be there and exceed expectations when an editor needs help, and you'll also find a far more receptive ear when you have something truly worthwhile to say on behalf of your company."
—Keith Larson, Vice President/Group Publisher,
Manufacturing Automation titles, Putman Media, Inc.

My first job out of college in 1981 was serving as the editorial assistant/secretary for a new arts magazine in Providence, Rhode Island. As the front desk person, I handled everything from walk-ins (which fortunately weren't many in what was an extremely unsavory part of town), to incoming mail, phone queries and followup. What an enlightenment!

Anyone overseeing or handling PR should work at a magazine or newspaper for just a few weeks. This will reinforce the concept that *the* most important factor to getting coverage in your target publication is knowing that the editor is your client. What does this mean? It means stepping inside their shoes. If you can't do it the way I did, with on-the-job experience, then fine-tune your empathy skills and see it from their perspective.

As the editorial assistant, I dealt with many people who wanted to get their article or artwork published in the magazine. Many tried to "strong-arm" me over the phone when they received their rejections in the mail. One gentleman called on behalf of his artist wife to ask angrily why we didn't publish her work in the magazine. Truth be told, her contribution was completely horrendous. But how do I tell the caller that the editor/publisher, a former dean at the Rhode Island School of Design (RISD), felt the artist's work wasn't of the caliber the magazine needed?

Another writer sent in poetry with a nicely written cover letter. Unfortunately, had she taken the time to read the publication, she would have realized that the magazine didn't publish poetry. It provided information and resources for artists, and was not a creative forum for literary works.

The submissions that did make it? The answer is very straightforward: those contributions that met the editor's needs. He was truly swamped with work and anything that made his job easier made the grade. The common characteristics:

- Typed (these were pre-computer days), brief cover sheets;
- Neatly produced slides (pre-jpeg days) of the artwork with clear captions;
- Strong professional credentials (artist had shown his/her work at different exhibits, and listed them in the cover letter);

■ Relevance to the publication's target audience and theme;

■ Good, solid contribution—nothing to raise the eyebrows or cause consternation on the editor's part;

■ No pestering follow-up calls (these were pre-e-mail days, in fact, even pre-answering machine days).

Although I was at the publication for less than a year, it was an eye-opener into the desperate foibles of the "outside world" and the popular misconceptions about publishing. The experience shaped my realization early on that an editor's job wasn't meant for me. While I loved working with words and seeing the magazine go from concept to final print each month, I knew I would become frustrated having to filter out the 80% of idiotic contributions in order to get to the 20% of intelligent submissions.

Too many executives are like those callers: viewing editors as eager little baby birds who are waiting for food from the "mama" company, ready to swallow the worm whole and not caring to discern what they're eating. In this type of approach, PR is synonymous with publicity, advertising, and brochures—all those kinds of communications in which you *do* have direct control over the message because it goes directly to the end user.

PR is a completely different communication vehicle, however, because of the editorial filter and go-between. If these same executives could change their mindsets and view themselves as providing services for the editor, instead of viewing the editor as a mere receptacle for their expressions and activities, they would truly achieve solid results.

Any good PR program will target the editor, not your end users. The editor takes your information, if it's prepared in the format he or she requires, and then filters it for the readers, who are your end users. If you try to create highly sensationalized documents that are more appropriate as brochures than as press releases or straightforward white papers, you will only turn the editor off.

If I had a nickel for every executive who felt strongly that the key to PR is to be aggressive, glitzy, strong-armed, and over the top, well…I would be living in Hawaii somewhere in a multi-million dollar house.

One reason executives feel this way may be that they often see their competitors painted in glowing terms in the vertical magazines. They make an understandable but erroneous assumption that all the competitor did was call up the editor, tell him what he or she wanted to have published, and voila!—instant coverage.

Unfortunately, they're missing the mental attitude and the crucial behind-the-scenes legwork that went into earning that positive coverage. The PR person probably approached the magazine in a methodical, ethical fashion, and over time (because PR *isn't* turned on like a faucet) reached a point with the editor where positive coverage ensued, both parties were happy, and neither felt manipulated. The following pages will guide you to similar outcomes, and yes, without manipulation!

Chapter 4:

Hiring the Right Person for Your Lead PR Position

"It is imperative to appoint an expert PR professional to appropriately manage all communication channels that reach the public eye. The PR expert can help mitigate legal risk factors as well as create a positive representation of the organization for multiple stakeholders. Ultimately, PR actions can impact the financial bottom-line of the business so it is crucial that these actions are of meticulous quality and completed only by a specialized PR practitioner."
—Lynne Habenicht, M.S., SPHR, hrFacets

If you are an executive, you have several choices available to you when you are looking to fill a PR opening at your company. You can promote someone from within, hire a full-time in-house person after reviewing resumes, or select a full-time outside agency. The first option is generally not recommended, and the second and third options are dependent upon the size of your company and your goals. Let's look at the first option.

Why not hire from within? Your argument may be that Robert or Susan has been with the company for several years (in another capacity) and has demonstrated eagerness and loyalty. You want to reward that loyalty with the promotion to PR Director. Do not confuse loyalty with talent, however. Just as you wouldn't promote someone from within to handle your legal counsel without a law degree, you shouldn't promote internally to the PR position unless the candidate has been trained in the field.

By moving an inexperienced, albeit willing, person into PR you degrade the profession by assuming that anyone who has a gift for gab or the ability to throw a fun party can and should take over the responsibility of communicating the corporate message to outside audiences. These audiences are sophisticated editors, analysts, and research specialists. In the days of increasing corporate oversight and transparency, you are playing with fire by securing the services of anyone who has not been trained formally in public relations.

The presence of a "newbie" within a corporation can be compared to that of a new crew member on a rowing team. The rest of the team has achieved synchronicity in its rowing efforts, moving the company steadily ahead and out of harm's way, ideally to reach the finish line ahead of the competition. With an inexperienced PR person on board, however, you have the equivalent of a new crew member who is more impressed with the fact that he or she is on the boat, waving to the passersby on shore, and exclaiming loudly that they now have an oar in hand (oh my!). You owe it to your executive team and corporate reputation not to travel this path.

Your second option is to hire a full-time PR person in-house, after reviewing external possibilities. Optimum routes to find that candidate include online resources such as monster.com or the local chapters of related professional associations, such as www.prsa.com (Public Relations Society of America) or www.iabc.com (International Association of Business Communicators). You can also check with colleagues in town and the editors of your local business papers or industry trade magazines to see whom they might recommend.

The benefit of an in-house director is that he or she will become intimately familiar with your corporate differentiators and goals, and knows how best to leverage that message to the right audiences. The upside is also that their annual salary will typically be less than the cost of an agency. The downside, however, is that they are not scalable.

Nonetheless, if your business employs fewer than 200 people and earns less than $20 million in annual revenues, you would be well served by employing in-house talent. If your business exceeds these general guidelines, however, you should consider hiring additional PR employees in-house reporting to the director, or securing the services of a PR agency.

The agency model brings with it the benefit of a full team that is scalable and ideally suited to launching big programs and/or multiple product lines. Agencies typically have an abundance of creative ideas because they have worked with so many different companies. The downside, however, is that you may be assigned a more junior person as your official company liaison, and the annual fees may be prohibitive, depending on the size of the agency. Local agencies average $5K – $15K monthly; the top names in the San Francisco or Boston area can be anywhere from $30K – $60K or more monthly.

Regardless of whether you choose in-house or agency, the top two criteria you should include in your evaluation are 1) experience and 2) chemistry. You want someone who has "been there, done that," and who fits in seamlessly with the personalities of your executive team.

There is a fourth option, and that is to hire a freelance public relations director. This route is best if you are a small start-up company that doesn't have the budget yet to employ a professional full-time, with all the required medical and social security benefits.

Or, you may be a large company with an in-house director who needs to supplement his or her services with dedicated support. Freelance professionals usually specialize in a certain market or niche, so you will get the benefit of someone who knows your market well, but at a pricepoint less than that of a full-time employee. The disadvantage is if you are a large and/or growing company who needs a comprehensive national or international campaign. In this instance, you should consider an agency.

Job Description

Once you've hired a PR director or agency, what should you expect them to do as part of their job description? The strategic goal of the position is to advance the positive, core messages of the corporation to its target editorial audiences. The position best accomplishes this if it is considered a key member of the executive team, and not a function to which management delegates tactical deliverables. You can't go wrong if you require the following key qualifications from your candidate:

- B.S. in journalism, mass communications or English

- Strong written and verbal communication skills

- In-depth understanding of public relations practices

- Ability to coordinate high volumes of work from diverse disciplines

The following are the numerous types of activities that come under the scope of the PR responsibility—note that press releases (company announcements) are just a portion of the total picture:

Crisis Public Relations

- Crisis PR plan
- Crisis reactions (layoff, employee injury, environmental problems)

Company Announcements

- Restructuring announcements
- New products
- Personnel appointments
- Donations
- Building expansions
- Third-party agreements, etc.

Editorial

- Article placement and editing
- Photo shoots for articles
- Corporate backgrounder
- Executive biographies
- Case studies
- White papers
- Editorial visits, both on company grounds and at magazine offices
- Industry analyst visits
- Editorial interviews
- Rebuttal letters and articles to defamatory claims
- Content for newsletters for media and customers
- Magazine supplements
- Books, ebooks, executive guides
- Company positioning on key industry issues
- Opinion essays
- Letters to the editor
- Executive and product photography
- Surveys

Corporate Support

- Speech writing and opportunities
- Annual report (non-financial data, in most cases)
- Some content for corporate videos (for corporate messaging)
- Trade show support
- International strategy and support
- PR plan as part of overall marketing plan

Miscellaneous Events

- Overseeing open houses
- Coordinating webcasts and podcasts
- Community participation (sponsorships, museum exhibits, high-tech career nights)

Administrative

- General inquiries from the community
- Directory and Buyer's Guide listings
- Award submission forms
- Clip sorting and distribution
- Reprints
- Budget and measurement

The most common mistakes executives make when hiring for public relations positions are hiring too junior a candidate in order to save on higher salary costs; hiring or promoting from within a candidate who has no formal training in the field; and not viewing the position as integral to the executive team. Ideally, the PR function should report directly to the CEO, rather than to a marketing communications director, vice president of marketing or vice president of sales. This ensures that the PR function can accurately reflect the company's mission and conduct mutually beneficial exchanges with the press. PR is the company's mirror to the rest of the market: choose carefully.

Chapter 5:

What to Include in a PR Plan

"Creating a marketing plan without a PR strategy is like architecting a house without knowing its location. So many critical factors influence the design of the house based upon where it is located, elevation, sight lines, etc. A successful marketing plan can only come together if the PR strategy complements, supports and reinforces all the marketing plan elements."
—Tom Blondi, CEO, Homefree

Now that you understand the importance of reaching an editorial audience, it's time for you to think about creating a PR plan for your product or service. Many executives avoid creating plans for fear they will prove baseless in a changing market, or that the plans will lock them unnecessarily into a roadmap for the future. Often, however, it is the exercise of assessing your company's strengths, the positioning of the competition, and your approach to undermine their position, that comprises the value of the plan. A PR plan also proves useful after you have hired a new employee in marketing, or an outside agency to help you with your plans. It shortens the learning curve and helps them understand the battlefield as well as the rationale for your strategy.

Most PR plans include the following components, and can be completed within two to four weeks of intensive study and research:

1. **Overview/Situation Analysis**—Is your company just beginning to play in its field, or is it a mature company that needs a turnaround? Where is the company in its growth stage? What resources and budgets are available at hand? Are there extenuating factors that will have implications for the PR program? What PR strategies have been tried in the past?

2. **Competitive/Market Analysis**—Who are the major players in this field, and how does your company stack up against them? What are its strengths and weaknesses? What are the market drivers and trends?

3. **Target Customers**—Which vertical markets are you selling your product to and what is the typical title of your intended customer? Will this target list stay the same over the next year, or expand to include new verticals?

4. **Strategies**—Is your strategy to promote the CEO as a spokesperson for the company? Is it to educate the customers about your services? Is it to penetrate a new market? Is it to position the company for an IPO or acquisition?

5. **Messages**—Based on the market trends, your company's situation, and the target customers, what specific messages should be aimed at each audience?

6. **Tactics**—What are the specific tactics you will employ in order to accomplish your strategies (e.g., press tours, webcasts, blogs, feature articles, white papers, charitable donations).

7. **Events**—Which events are part of the marketing strategy and will require PR support or participation (e.g. trade shows, user conferences, webcasts, speaking opportunities)?

8. **Primary Media Contacts**—What list of analysts and media, as well as local community contacts, will be in your media database? Have you verified that these are the right contacts and that they wish to be on the distribution list?

9. **Editorial Calendar/Awards**—Based on the published editorial calendars of the magazines that serve your markets, what opportunities are coming up in the year that tie into your company themes and products? Are there key industry awards that you plan to apply for?

10. **Budget and Measurement**—What expenses do you foresee for the year, and how and when do you plan to measure your effectiveness? Will you conduct a baseline study in the beginning, with followup studies throughout the year?

11. **Conclusion**—What is the summary of the plan's intent and scope?

Chapter 6:

The Media Database: How to Find Those Names

"The key to driving media placement is to understand what the media want. What your organization does is important, but not as important as determining how it will fit into a writer's article parameters. Public relations professionals should equip themselves with in-depth editorial placement research, in order to pitch with relevance and accuracy—the essentials for building credibility and generating 'ink.'"
—Steve Smith, Managing Director, PRSourceCode LLC

A large part of the success of any PR campaign is making certain that the critical information is being delivered to the right people, before you even craft your message. The right people are those editors, analysts, consultants and other "influencers" who are interested in your market and have the potential to write articles that will sway your customers. But how do you find that magic list?

Many agencies, because they are pressed for time and handle public relations for multiple clients, resort to online services or subscription-based software packages. These services allow you to search for editors in a particular market, such as retail, real estate, technology, and so on. Once this list is compiled, it is imperative not to neglect to query the editors and consultants on that list first. In this way, you make sure that the media actually are the correct ones covering that beat, and that they do indeed want to hear from company XYZ. Instead, many inexperienced PR specialists will send the announcements off to the entire database, and are surprised when the editors respond tersely or not at all!

While there are time savings and value to these online services, there are challenges as well. It can be difficult to query online because many publications do not fit neatly into one category or another. Complicating the research process further is that in some instances, unless you know the name of the magazine, you may miss including it on your list entirely, or unless you've read the magazine personally, you won't realize that it's a good target. The cost may be prohibitive as well, unless you are a large agency that can split the cost among several clients. Finally, many online services are only updated periodically, although they have made more of an effort in recent years to improve the 'real-time' nature of the data.

So how to compile the list? Good old block-and-tackle PR research skills are the best method. This approach works most effectively if you have an in-house PR capability or are focusing on just a few clients or markets. Begin by collecting all the magazines that serve your market. The engineers and executives in the company are probably already receiving many of the top magazines on that list. There is also a very helpful hard copy directory from Bacon's (see Resource Directory at the end of this book) that divides publications by category. You just flip to the section you want, and note the various publications in that category. If you want to get as narrow as "Kentucky Golfer," there are indeed print publications that are that focused.

Continue to expand the starter list: read, read, read everything in the industry to get a feel for the trends covered. Anytime you see an editor or analyst quoted in a feature article, use a search engine and find out their location and contact information. Do query them first before adding them to your master list, however—make sure they want to hear from you!

Another fast method of finding out who the key influencers are in your market is to peruse the website newsroom section of your competitors. There is usually an area on their website where they list recent magazine coverage or analyst quotes. This will provide you with a good idea of which magazines and analyst groups they target in their PR efforts.

For large, multinational corporations, it may be important also to include broadcast media in your list, but for the purposes of this book, the focus is on print publications.

Building a complete database takes several months of effort; getting to know the market, reading the key magazines, and going through directories. Using a one-stop online service may be one way to jumpstart your list, but shouldn't be the beginning and end of your research efforts.

Blogs have a place in your database as well, although they are more difficult to locate. Bloggers are often journalists for classic media as well, and once you find their blogs you can reach them through the "back door" of the blog. Several services, such as bloglines (www.bloglines.com) aggregate blogs and present a searchable format. Once you find a blogger, however, don't ever send him/her a press release. This is not good etiquette for the bloggersphere, says Francine Hardaway, former PR executive at Intel and long-time blogger (http://blog.stealthmode.com).

Once you have compiled those names, enter them into a solid Customer Relationship Management (CRM) package such as ACT!. The benefit of a traditional CRM package over a spreadsheet is that querying and creating groups is much faster and easier in a full-featured package that is specifically designed for relationship-building, not financial applications. You may find that you want to create subgroups within your markets. For example, "oil and gas editors," and "refining editors" would be placed under the larger umbrella group of "editors serving the chemical market." This enables you to send releases to just those groups of editors who will be interested, not to a mass email group.

You can use the database capabilities to easily mail/merge correspondence with the editors, as well as keep track of when you contacted them and how often. Work the list in order to build an ongoing relationship with the editors—not simply for the purpose of shoving information down their throats.

If your company is publicly held or has plans for a future IPO, another entity in your PR database should be the research or financial analysts at the investment houses. Finding these can be somewhat trial and error, but it is often helpful to check with the company CFO. Usually the research analysts find them first, so they can keep current with the company's progress, particularly if they sense it is edging towards an IPO.

Other categories of media interested in your company's activities include local newspapers and business journals, chambers of commerce, trade/entrepreneurial organizations, and university professors. Your local business publication will often include mentions of and/or contributed articles from these groups.

Finally, you may want to add the advertising sales reps at the magazines where your advertising manager buys media. Keeping them abreast of your company developments may help them recognize future advertising and editorial opportunities that tie into your themes. Much has been written about the separation between advertising and editorial; over time, these lines have blurred, arguably for good or bad.

Ultimately, the number of entries in your media list can vary greatly. Lists can be as small as 50 or as large as 300.

Quantity is not always synonymous with quality, however. Do not be over-impressed with huge press lists in the thousands.

Sometimes agencies will pad lists with multiple editors or report-ers from one publication, but in most cases, you only need one contact from each publication. Lists that have over 300 names are generally filled with editors who are not interested in your prod-uct or service, and who will be genuinely irritated to receive your announcement. The exception is if you have a product that appeals to the wide consumer audience in multiple markets. Better to err on the side of caution than to believe that the "shot-gun" effect will have any solid results. The foot you shoot will most likely be your own.

Chapter 7:

The Company Backgrounder and Executive Bios

"It may be difficult to condense the work of a lifetime into a company backgrounder, or executive biography, but it must be done. Editors are looking to provide succinct differentiators, often comparing and contrasting the work of companies that on the surface may appear quite similar. Given deadline pressures, it's also true that editors tend to take the line of least resistance. If a high-quality backgrounder or biography is put in front of them, they're just that much more likely to use it."
—Kevin Parker, Editorial Director,
Manufacturing Business Technology magazine

A difficult task I've had as a consultant is convincing clients of the importance of a corporate backgrounder as the first step in the creation of company materials. This document ideally should be written before any other information on the business is created. Why? It's the pithy summary of what your company is all about, and any editor looking for information on your website is going to head first to the company backgrounder. It's the PR equivalent of turning the key in the ignition of a car before the car can move forward.

One of the best backgrounders I ever read was written in 1985 by the PR department of Sun Microsystems. Until then, much of the technology industry was dominated by minicomputer companies that loved their technical jargon. Sun came along in the mid '80s and revolutionized high-tech marketing by using photos of their workstations in a "Santa Fe"-type environment—a complete change from the typical stiff "engineer-sitting-at-a-keyboard" look that was popular at the time.

Sun also took pains to write their company description about open standards in as clear terms as possible. Everything about their approach was clean, fresh, factual, and enlightening. I saved that backgrounder, and it is just as concise today as it was over 20 years ago.

Most executives are too far down the tunnel of information about their company to connect with the people at the entrance: i.e., those unfamiliar with the terrain. In other words, executives are so immersed in the day-to-day jargon of their business that they have trouble achieving perspective and clarity. A good PR person has the ability to bridge both worlds: the client he/she is representing, and the target media audience. Communication is critical to success. And the backgrounder is the *de rigueur* form of providing that information in an easy-to-digest format for the media.

Corporate backgrounders can vary from industry to industry, but in general, they should contain the following components:

- Press contact for further information
- Brief (2-3 sentence) summary of what the company does
- Status (privately or publicly held, stock ticker symbol)
- Key markets served, and market overview and explanation (very helpful to editors new to their beat)
- Any major partnerships/distributorships

- Senior management (CEO, CTO, CFO, VP Marketing, VP Sales, VP Human Resources, VP Services)

- Domestic and international sales offices

- Product overview (brief summaries—you can always include details in separate data sheets or a separate technical backgrounder)

- Any major awards or distinctions

- List of top customers in each major market the company serves, and installed base (how many customers and educational institutions are using the product or service)

- Corporate history if the company is more than a year or two old (providing a history for anything less than that can appear a bit presumptuous, not to mention over-eager)

- Corporate philosophy (Sun's press backgrounder, for example, had a section entitled, "Open Systems: The Sun Approach")

- Board of directors and advisors

- Future plans

- Address, phone, website of the company

Executive Bios

It's a good idea to complete the executive biographies at the same time that you write the company backgrounder. Some backgrounders include the bios; in other cases, it's more important to separate them, particularly if yours is a big company and the list of executives is lengthy.

Editors read this information to understand your company's experience and its range of talent. If you have management with strong industry experience, this is an ideal place to showcase them.

Their bios could read something like this:

David A. Bennett
Chief Technology Officer

Dave is Axway's technology visionary, widely acclaimed for his business technology views and accomplishments. For over 20 years, he has focused exclusively on integration and messaging-oriented applications. He has designed and developed distributed systems for banking, retail, and supply chain execution using wireless, IP, satellite, ASYNC, SNA, B2B, EAI, and P2P technologies. Prior to Axway, Dave founded Cyclone Commerce, Inc., one of the leading providers of B2B technologies, which was acquired by Sopra Group in January 2006, and Dave was named CTO of the software subsidiary, Axway, Inc. His background also includes positions as an engineering and technical services executive for Gateway Data Sciences Corporation and as vice president of engineering and operations for Nations Bank and American Express while living in Japan. His education includes several technical certifications in development and networking, and he earned a B.S. degree in computer science from DeVry University.

Be sure to include top-quality digital photography for this section. Unfortunately, this is an area where many companies try to cut costs, and the poor executive ends up silhouetted against a plain background, looking miserable. A professionally done photo is part of the total "image" that you want to portray. Grainy, poorly shot photos equate to a poorly run company in the media's mind. It suggests that if you're scrimping *here*, where else are you scrimping? In your customer service? In your product design? Having a list of stellar executive bios and not including good quality photos to accompany them is like showing up at your wedding in a tuxedo and a pair of sneakers. No one remembers the tuxedo or your other great qualities, but they do remember the silly sneakers.

Chapter 8:

Why on Earth Do You Need a Website?

"Your website is your company's real-time Curriculum Vitae. Just as you would screen a candidate, your audience is screening you through this dynamic medium and you've got about 7 seconds to pass muster. I'd trade all of my printed material for an engaging website. It's alive, it's current, it's the encapsulation of your company's persona and value proposition in 1.3 million pixels."
—Gene Wang, Chairman and CEO, Bitfone, Inc.

For those of us accustomed to tried-and-true methods of marketing such as brochures, trade shows, personal relationships or press releases, the hoopla surrounding websites can seem like the latest Barnum & Bailey circus. It comes into town with a lot of sound and fury and leaves after a short while. A fad by any other name is still a fad.

But websites are no transient visitor to the world of marketing. There's a lot of rationale behind including a strong website in your arsenal of communication tools.

Many of the reasons may not be immediately apparent if you've been focusing on brochures or word-of-mouth in the past, or if you personally don't visit websites of companies when you research information for your own benefit. You're probably prone to thinking, "If I'm not using the Internet to get information, most of my customers aren't either." Or you may be fearful of revealing too much information to your competitors via an easily accessible medium such as a website. I've also met clients who don't feel they need to boast about their capabilities and feel self-conscious getting dressed up for a photo shoot.

To understand why websites are important, you have to remember that the world is made up of different kinds of people and different ways to access information. Some people are aurally oriented—they like to speak with people over the phone and receive information that way. Some like the personal one-on-one meetings and forging relationships and obtaining data that particular way. There is still another group that is somewhat reticent, albeit industrious, that prefers to conduct their research via print at their own convenience. This last group is important to remember when you prepare your marketing strategy.

There are both customers and a majority of busy editors who prefer to obtain information about your services via a non-intrusive, 24x7 medium such as a website. By not including the correct content in a website, you're effectively eliminating 25-40 percent of your target audience right off the bat. Do you want to neglect such an important sector of people who can buy or influence others to buy your product?

While you may personally not be prone to using the Internet, there are many, particularly younger buyers and editors, who grew up on computers and can't imagine any other way. These are the people who will go to what they perceive to be the best website in order to make a purchase or obtain background information for an article. Their rationale will be, "If Company A has so little content on its website, and makes it so difficult for me to find the information I want, then I'll go to Company B, because their website is easier to navigate and has a lot more information, so it's probably a better indicator of the successful company they are."

To come up with the content and navigational methods for your website, it's helpful both to review what other companies inside and outside of your market are doing, and to take the time to examine the demographics of your target customers. What kinds of information do your buyers want and need to know? Is it pricing? Is it the range of services/products available?

Following are some minimal required components to successful websites:

- Information about your range of products and/or services

- Key features of each product and/or service

- Upcoming events where your company may be participating/speaking/exhibiting

- Sales offices

- List of partners/resellers

- A clearly defined "Newsroom" where press announcements, case studies and articles are contained

- A clearly defined contact list for media inquiries, sales inquiries, and technical support

- Company background information

- Information about the executive team

In addition, it is helpful to include an area on your website where visitors can contact the company with questions. If you can include an e-commerce component so that visitors can purchase your product or order your services from the website using a credit card, you've improved your chances of increased revenue immensely. You might also consider hosting an interactive survey on your site connected to your industry or product and publicize the results.

Don't make the mistake of trying to save money and creating the website on your own. In this Internet age, the homegrown websites stand out as painful indications of the lack of interest and budget on their company's part. Is this the message you want to convey to customers and the media?

To design information for an electronic world requires website design skills that very few people have—the likelihood is, you weren't born both with a talent for design and for running your business. Just as you wouldn't expect a designer to excel in your world, don't put the same expectations on your own design capabilities. Hire an expert.

Some people are reluctant to include corporate information such as executive teams or pricing on their website. By being this cloistered, however, you are missing the larger picture—a huge customer and editor population—by failing to provide this information.

Many people believe that if you don't include more detailed product or service information, then the company is doing something clandestine, or alternatively, you are so small and inconsequential that you don't have enough activity or substance. Most people aren't patient, and will go to the next best competitor. As for the competition trying to steal away your executives, maybe it's time to focus on what your company needs to do to attract and retain good talent. It doesn't always boil down to a higher salary, as studies have shown.

Editors need to know who is on your team. The website is also a good way to demonstrate to customers the range of experience and talent behind the company brand. The big players in manufacturing and technology didn't get to their current leadership positions by hiding their light under a bushel. Don't make the same mistake in your own marketing efforts—be sure your website is the best reflection of your company's image.

Website? The Who and the What

So you've finally decided to create or update your website to make it more appealing to editors. Great! Now what?

Like any other new project, creating your first web page can be confusing. Here are some steps to easing the process of finding a web designer and creating a website:

Finding a web designer:

Networking can be a great way to find the perfect web designer. Do any of your business acquaintances or friends have great websites? Ask who designed their site.

Surf the Internet. If you find a site that has the style and flair that you're going for, look at the bottom of the index page—most web designers put their company name with a link to their site at the bottom of their client's opening web page. Although it's sometimes helpful to find someone local, you can hire anyone, anywhere; distance is not usually a factor.

Use search engines. If you feel more comfortable hiring a local web designer, go to any of the major search engines and type "web design (your city)." This should bring up quite a few choices. Any good web designer will have several examples of their work. Narrow down the field to those designers who can provide examples of the structure, artistic abilities, and professional look that you want for your own site.

A good web designer should:

- **Ask what *you* need**, rather than trying to up-sell you on expensive additions that don't serve your goals. Flash, ASP, databases and e-commerce are up-sells for basic business websites.

■ **Help you find a web host** to house your website. If the designer does not offer a web hosting package, he or she should be more than happy to help you find something to suit your needs.

■ **Design fast-loading pages** that will appear, in entirety, within three seconds of being opened. Any longer than that and you risk losing potential clients.

■ **Write meta tags** for each and every page so search engines will be able to catalog your site. Meta tags are what search engines "read" to know what's on each page. Without this information, search engines will skip over you; in turn your web pages won't show up when clients look for your subject matter.

■ **Include search engine submission** with the cost of the design. Although monthly re-submission is necessary to rise in the rankings, designers should make the initial submission of your site for you.

■ **Include one contact form and pictures**. You should not be charged extra for one contact form on your site or for one to four pictures per page. Adding more pictures might require an additional fee, but you shouldn't need to pay for a minimal amount of pictures per page.

■ **Provide a bottom-line cost,** with no hidden fees. Any reputable designer will provide a contract with a breakdown of the number of pages, what all will be included, and the total cost. Services and design shouldn't be left up in the air.

■ **Allow at least one revision** for any changes you need made to the design, pictures or text. Many designers will allow you opportunities to preview your site several times for revisions, so the final site will be exactly what you want.

Chapter 9:

So the Competition is Eating Your Lunch? How to Take Them On

"No amount of business is worth losing your integrity or credibility in the marketplace. Integrity is job #1 when it comes to taking on the competition in your market space. Too many companies forget to focus on their unique strengths, and instead try to issue press releases that are specifically geared towards competing vendors. As an industry analyst group, we prize companies who can articulate their differentiators without bashing the competition."
—Andy Chatha, President, ARC Advisory Group

It will inevitably arise, that sense of profound irritation when you see a competitor beating you at your own game. You see them mentioned everywhere, in all the major industry magazines, in analyst reports, and in advertisements. Their product is inferior to yours, they've stolen your tagline and made it their own, and they have managed to steal your thunder. What to do?

The natural human reaction is to fight back to reclaim your territory. You instinctively want the media to know and understand that *your* company was first in this market. *Your* product and customer service are the best. If you could only convince them of the plain truth of your claims. You tell yourself that you must launch a direct attack!

The way to beat your competition, however, is not to resort to primitive instincts that are more applicable to Cro-Magnon Man than to a modern executive. You and your company will only look plaintive and whiny, not to mention primeval. Trying to fight back in this manner does so from a point of weakness. After all, your competitor has staked a claim in the market. Your goal, therefore, is not to resort to the old "My Dad is bigger than your Dad" kind of fight. You need to move the battle to your own turf, where the competition can't compete.

What does that mean? You need to create an environment in which your company's natural strengths are obvious. You position the company as strong, credible, fair-minded, and nimble. You're above the fray and the antics of your competition. Your ego is not invested, and therefore the company appears stronger.

In order to stop the competition from eating your lunch, you have to spend time isolating what your company's top two strengths are. (This is normally identified early on through the creative process of the overall marketing plan, but admittedly not everyone takes this chronological approach). Maybe it's quality of product, maybe it's your small, nimble size and top customer service. Regardless of what your true strengths are, identify them.

Let's say for example that you're up against a company that has been in the industry for 20 years, a behemoth of longevity, particularly in industries such as high-tech. But your company was formed because the behemoth was falling behind the times, reacting slowly to change, a virtual Titanic that was impossible to turn around quickly.

Your company's strengths, in contrast, are innovation of product and responsiveness to market changes. Your CEO is bright and engaging, not a semi-retired executive looking for the nearest golf course. You haven't been in the industry for 20 years (past), but you are more in tune with where the industry is headed (future).

Now that you've identified your key differentiators, create a strategy of integrated marketing communications (remember, PR does not act alone) to consistently promote those differentiators. The following are some tactics described in this book that you can successfully use and which, over time, will propel you to top mindshare with the editors and analysts. From a PR standpoint, this is your goal: to educate them about your accurate differentiators in a fair, ethical, and practical manner. You will incorporate:

- Survey/real-world data
- Website content
- White papers
- Webcast
- Press releases
- Press tour
- Customer case studies
- Consigned third-party paper (written by an analyst in the industry)

The above tactics are much more successful (and much more sophisticated!) than trying to take on the competition in chest-beating wordplay. You're creating your own fight based on reality, not merely reacting to what the competition is doing. By reacting, you only accomplish two unworthy goals: you add credence to the competition's claims, and you create a negative impression of your company as a bit player in the behemoth's industry. Don't fall into your competitor's trap.

Chapter 10:

How to Handle an Analyst Tour

---

*"CEOs can learn several lessons about how successful ana-
lyst-client relationships should be modeled. First, they should
tailor their presentation and expectations for the meeting to
what would be valuable to the analyst. Second, they should
be willing to share their market understanding and other
intellectual property. And third, they need to remember analysts are in business to make money."*
— Cushing Anderson, Research Director,
    IDC Software Strategic Alliance

One of the best ways to promote your company's strengths is
to establish give-and-take relationships with industry analyst groups
and/or smaller consulting groups and individuals. If you are a
CEO, you may think you already know how to work with the
industry analysts, but my experience has been that very few CEOs
truly "get it."

The problem is they often view the relationship as a one-way
process: feeding marketing propaganda to the analysts, instead of
sharing real-world data and seeking corporate direction in return.

Too many executives think of contacting the analyst *after* the product launch, for example, instead of before a single line of code is written.

As Gartner Research Vice President Dale Vecchio explains, "Analysts are not customers. Don't present to them as if they are! Analysts need to understand more than what's presented in traditional sales presentations and marketing slides. They need to understand enough to put your solutions in perspective with your competitors and customer needs. Industry analysts need to understand your strategy, message and ability to deliver on both."

The key to successful analyst relationships is partnership. Think of the analyst as a close brother/sister or perhaps a best friend. They should know everything going on in your life (company) and represent one of the first people you think of when you're about to make an important decision, such as whom to marry (partner with) or what to wear to the prom (how to package your product). If you can think in these terms, you're on the road to success.

Admittedly, the tricky part is treading carefully around an executive's sense of self, as he/she usually earns the position of chief executive officer by virtue of an assertive, ego-driven style that appeals to boards of directors. This style is usually anathema to analysts, however. CEOs may walk away from an industry analyst meeting thinking, "Wow, I really impressed that guy" when in fact the analyst has been sending covert facial signals throughout the hour that the CEO is an embarrassing blowhard. Whereas the CEO's job, as he perceives it, is to keep board members feeling comfortable that they made the right decision by appointing him, with analysts he needs to approach the relationship differently and use the analyst as a neutral sounding board in order to *reach* the right decisions for the future of the company. Big difference.

Some major tips for handling industry analyst tours:

1. **One size doesn't fit all**. Tailor the preparation specifically for an analyst audience, not for media or financial analysts. In the rush to set up a media tour, usually the media, industry analysts and financial analysts are all lumped together and receive one PowerPoint "data dump" of information that is tailored to everyone and serves no one. Industry analysts really aren't as interested in how much you'll make in revenues—they tend not to believe those inflated scales anyway. Don't tell them the market size—that's their job. They each have their own market sizing methodology, so use the meeting to seek their input on what they think the market parameters are.

2. **Use PowerPoint slides as a leave-behind, not as a presentation tool**. Give the analysts a break. How would you like to politely sit through presentation after presentation until you're bleary-eyed from repetition? While it may be heady to pontificate to a captive audience, it's torture for an analyst to hear yet another executive start off with the same company info in the same sequence. Sit down with the analyst and carry on a conversation. There is no strict agenda—just back and forth sharing of information. This doesn't mean you should go in unprepared, but have the data committed to memory so the information flows freely and at the appropriate time, instead of by some pre-scripted formula. Then give the analyst the PowerPoint file or printout as a leave-behind to document the key points that were probably covered in the discussion.

3. **Dress appropriately**. East coast analysts, particular those in Boston, favor navy blue suits and red ties. California analysts are a little more relaxed, but usually a suit and tie are pretty safe. The cute dotcom days of touring with a hip 20-year-old CEO in jeans or khakis are over.

4. **Force yourself to participate in a dry run with a local analyst first or better yet, undergo media training**. Your instincts may fight you, and you believe that you have done "hundreds" of these meetings before. The quantity is irrelevant. It's important to do them right. If you won't concede to media training, at least start off the tour with the analyst or group that you feel will have the least impact on your company. That way, you're using those first meetings as a dry run before the big event.

5. **Share your own market data**. It's easy to forget that the analysts aren't always the ones with the data. Your company has access to valuable "real world" customer information that can be shared informally with the analysts from time to time, as well as during the actual tour. Examples include any feedback from your customer service organization on how users are responding to a product—what types of calls come in the most often, for example. What region of the country are most of your customers based in and why are you reaching them? What percentage of your customers feel a certain way about a hot issue in the industry?

6. **After the tour, determine which group/analyst is the best fit and enter a subscription with them**. Don't make the mistake of meeting with them on a tour and not dancing with any of them afterwards. An analyst's time is valuable and they have many companies to cover and miles of paperwork to assimilate before they go to sleep. After a tour, you should have a good idea of which individual or group has the best chemistry as well as the best market sense.

7. **Read this chapter over before going on an analyst tour**. Ask the analysts, and they'll regale you with stories of executives on analyst tours—"kittens with new claws" who are more concerned with impressing the analysts than seeking

feedback. If you personally feel that a particular analyst isn't smart enough to understand your company's product/service, that's usually another warning sign. My dad used to say, "If someone can't catch a ball, it's usually the fault of the person throwing it." If your company's messaging is truly on target, the analysts are experienced enough to know what will fly and what won't. They are exposed to more competitive market information than one executive can ever be. You might not be conveying the message properly, or an even scarier thought, the company's mission may be out of step with market trends. Either way, it indicates a real need to partner with that analyst to refine the company's presentation and business direction.

Those are some tips for a successful analyst tour. There's plenty you can do after the tour as well, such as scheduling periodic teleconferences to seek analysts' input or flying them out to your corporate site. The first impression, however, is usually the most important one.

Chapter 11:

What to Include in a Press Release

"One of the biggest misconceptions that companies have about press releases is believing that everyone in the world should receive their press release. It's more practical to segment your audience, by vertical market or geographical region, for example, to get the best bang for the buck."
— Tony Bracanovich, Regional Account Manager, PrimeNewsWire

According to *Webster's New World Dictionary,* a press release is "a statement or story prepared for release to the news media." Therein lies the problem that many companies have when they prepare a news release. They write them as if they were designing marketing brochures to be handed to the end user, and forget that the medium is really intended for an editorial audience first, not a consumer audience. Sticking to the original intention of news release formats will help you write releases that are picked up, not ignored, by the media.

You may see other companies going for the sensational, promotional type of press release writing style. Don't worry! The media won't pick these up and are more than likely going out of their way to ignore the company that practices this technique. Just because you see press releases written in this style does not mean the editors receive them with warmth and admiration.

One client's press release, for example, described a recent trade show they had attended. Visitors to the event, we were told in the copy, were "agog with delight and curiosity" about the client's booth. These phrases, however, are more appropriate for movie reviews than press releases.

Basic Press Release Components

In general, releases should include the following standard components:

- *Company logo, location, and contact information*— Remember, many of the editors you send your release to will not be familiar with your company or where it's located, so include that info on the electronic submission. If you still are using hard copy, print the release on company letterhead and just key in "News Release" across the top right hand portion of the page. There is no need to order special paper just for news releases.

- *Contact information that can be easily found*—It's helpful to put the contact information at the beginning or top of the press release, including name, work number, cell phone number, and email address of the person who is responsible for handling media inquiries. Some companies include the information at the end, but the editor may not read your release all the way through.

- *Headline*—Decide what you are announcing, and make the headline clear: "XYZ Masonry Hires Susan Doe as President"; or "ABC Masonry Announces New Capabilities for Residential Builders."

■ **Subhead that summarizes the focus of the release**—This subhead should really hit the hot buttons of the announcement: what are the implications, benefits and ramifications of the announcement? If you're announcing a new service, what succinct benefit does it provide the customer? If you have a new president, what is she or he chartered to do? Is your company taking a new strategic direction?

■ **Dateline**—Editors work on deadlines and like to compile information that is fresh. Include a "dateline" on every release, one that mentions the date and the city or town where your company is issuing the announcement. If it's from company headquarters, use the headquarters city. If it's issued during a trade show at which you're exhibiting, you can use the location of the trade show itself.

■ **Body**—This is perhaps the area that most companies trip up on. In the first paragraph, try to include as much as possible of the "who/what/where/why/when," so that an editor need only read the first few lines to get the "meat" of the announcement. If you're announcing a partnership with another company, or a recent customer win, it's helpful to include a brief, informative quote from the other partner or company. Try to make the quote meaningful and descriptive of what the customer's perspective is.

Remember, however, that most quotes are not taken seriously by editors because they suspect (and in 85 percent of the instances they are probably correct) that the vendor created the quote for the customer in order to make themselves look good.

Include straightforward detail about the announcement you're making. If you have a new service, when is it available? Does it replace other services? How much does it cost? What will it help customers do? Try to think like a detective who has to write a complete synopsis based only on the information you provide in the release. Anticipate the questions you'd have if a competitor of yours had an announcement. What would you want to know? Press releases are public documents, not sales hype, so this is not the time to be cagey or coy. Spell it out.

- *Company boilerplate or bio*—These company descriptions are located at the end of every release and range from beautifully brief to Ph.D.-dissertation long. Aim for the "30-second elevator speech" description if you can. Microsoft's boilerplate, for example, is simply, "Founded in 1975, Microsoft (Nasdaq "MSFT") is the worldwide leader in software, services and solutions that help people and businesses realize their full potential."

- *Trademarks*—If your company name and/or products and services have trademarks, include them at the very end of the release. Remember, only you can protect your trademark or copyright.

- *Tags and links*—These are fairly recent developments in press releases. According to Juan De Leon, communications research manager at the Eastwick agency, "Using links and tags in press release copy improves the ranking and relevancy in search engines such as Yahoo and Google and therefore better visibility to end audiences—those people who would be most interested in the news."

He defines links as a reference in hypertext systems such as the World Wide Web to references in another document. Such links are sometimes called "hot links" because they take you to another document when you click on them.

Tags, he notes, are keywords that describe the content of a website, bookmark, photo or blog post. You can assign multiple tags to the same online resource, and different people can assign different tags to the same resource. They provide a useful way of organizing, retrieving and discovering information.

Writing Style: Follow the 10K

Now that you know what to include, what should you know about writing style? If you ask editors what they dislike most about the press releases they receive, their answers are consistent. They don't like copy that is full of hackneyed superlatives, such as "leading provider," "state-of-the-art technology." If you want to see what good informative copy can read like, take any large company's 10K form and try to emulate the tone. It represents a neutral reporting style that conveys important messages in an enlightening manner without sounding like a circus hawker with a microphone.

If you try to think of press releases as narrative, legal documents that briefly announce a milestone or event, you'll significantly increase your chances of getting your company noticed by the media. They'll remember you for your brevity and appreciate you for your straightforwardness.

Note: A Word About Style and Endings

It's a good idea to pick up a copy of the *AP (Associated Press) Stylebook* or *Chicago Manual of Style* if you're the one who will be responsible for writing press releases. These valuable guides provide examples of how certain phrases and punctuation should be handled in a press release going to the media. Among the most common mistakes are inappropriate capitalization of titles and nouns and incorrect punctuation placement. The following are some examples:

RIGHT: Linda VandeVrede, president of VandeVrede Public Relations, said…

WRONG: Linda VandeVrede, President of VandeVrede Public Relations (president should not be capitalized), said….

RIGHT: "The product is priced at $595," said VandeVrede.

WRONG: "The product is priced at $595", said VandeVrede. (comma should come before the quotation marks)

Confused about whether it's northwestern U.S. or Northwestern U.S.? Pick up the handbook. (OK, the answer is, Northwestern U.S.)

The end of press releases used to include -30-, which was an old typesetting mark used to indicate the end of the text. Today, most press releases end with ### or nothing at all. Public companies include the standard "safe harbor" verbiage at the end of every release, which you can find on any public company's website on the Internet.

Chapter 12:

Press Releases Are
Not a PR Strategy

"...there are several fronts on which you must launch a coordinated attack to be successful. The more carefully planned your communications efforts are, the more likely they will support your marketing objectives. It is not necessarily those with the best ideas who succeed—it is those who best communicate their ideas."
>   —Frances Emerson, Vice President,
>   Corporate Communications and
>   Global Brand Management, Deere & Company

There seems to be a powerful misconception in the business world that public relations is composed simply of press releases— that a so-called "PR strategy" is sending out announcements as often as possible.

Unfortunately, the overwhelming majority of businessmen and women, from neophyte to seasoned executive, equate PR with press releases. The terms are interchangeable, in their minds. No wonder editors want to barricade their virtual (email) doors from the vendors, who are as fast and misguided as the attacking zombies in "Dawn of the Dead." Instead of trying to overcome their prey with fatal bites, companies are "biting" the life and patience out of editors by jamming the electronic wires with press releases. In most instances, management is instructing their PR departments to send out releases as the official PR strategy out of ignorance, not realizing that focusing solely on this one tactic has an adverse impact on the company overall.

First we need to understand where this prevailing misconception came from. Most likely it's the deceptive nature of PR. The uninformed see press releases, then read a write-up in the paper later, and think, "Oh, *that's* how you get coverage. You need to send out a release, and the more releases you send out, *the more* coverage you get, or at least the greater chance of getting picked up."

Why is PR not press releases? Well, press releases are merely one tiny arrow in a very full quiver of tools that should be implemented as part of an overall strategy. Moreover, they are probably *one of the least effective*, simply because everyone thinks they can write them, and they distribute them to excess. There is a certain approach to writing press releases and executives don't understand it. They use them inappropriately as promotional mini-brochures, thinking they are the first ones to be so clever as to write the copy to influence editors and to issue them at periodic two-week intervals. Sadly, that is like thinking you are the first Columbus if you arrived on American soil in 1992, instead of 1492.

PR is also not press releases because it's an insult to think you should or could frame an editor's insight merely by writing down your best persuasive expression and sending it off. Think, instead, of all the different methods by which a person might reach an educated decision.

Other tools in the arsenal are scheduling one-on-one meetings with the editors…providing beta site statistics…supplying real-world information the editors might not otherwise be able to get such as customer service specs or feedback...when appropriate, sending them a sample of the product so they can test it out on their own...writing a white paper that explains (in academic, straightforward terms!) your company's stand on a particular issue, or a best practices approach to a common problem facing your target markets...holding a webcast that features industry pundits and your best customers...conducting a survey of customers and parlaying that into solid data for the analysts and reporters...presenting a speech on how your company solved a particular problem...crafting an article that takes a new approach on a popular topic...submitting a sidebar to a feature article that provides an opposing view...creating a customized graphic that explains a complex concept in simple terms...the list goes on.

All of these tactics become part of the larger PR strategy, which always should be to increase awareness of your company's inherent (not blown out of proportion) strengths and clear market advantages.

PR is not press releases. It is not spin. It is not manipulation. And unless things change in the business world, it is not being conducted properly. Take a look at the "editorial guidelines" of any high-profile publication and you'll quickly realize the detrimental effect of conventional views of PR on the profession. It's time to shake ourselves out of this zombie-like state of dead-wrong reckoning.

Chapter 13:

Case Studies, Articles and White Papers

"Seeing is believing! Readers (potential customers) love to see 'real world' examples of the proven benefits of a particular product and/or service before they buy it themselves. Case studies provide the right problem/solution format to stream-line this decision-making process."
—Frank Benassi, Senior Features Editor,
Standard & Poor's

Case studies, articles and white papers are very effective public relations vehicles for communicating your corporate mes-sage. Here is an explanation of how each should be written and applied:

Case Studies

Case studies, also called testimonials, are simply summaries of how your key customers are using your product or service. The typical format describes what problem the end user faced, the evaluation process they used to consider various solutions, what the final configuration included, and results and/or benefits. When completed, the case studies can be used in a variety of ways, from postings on your website to submissions to industry magazines or as a component of your sales materials. To avoid problems and to streamline the writing and approval process, the following guidelines are recommended:

1. If your company has not prepared case studies before, issue an announcement from the company CEO or vice president of sales to sales force and industry managers that their job performance will be rated on how much they cooperate with public relations on identifying, reviewing, and following up on customer success stories and working closely with the assigned writers. Unless you motivate the sales and marketing team, they will drag their feet.

2. Establish PR as a single point of contact for case studies. Any and all inside and external writers should report into that person.

3. The industry manager and/or sales rep should first identify the opportunity.

4. The PR director mails or faxes an authorization form to the customer that includes the request and information about how the final approved story will be used (see sample in this chapter).

5. Once the customer has signed off and faxed back the form, the industry manager and sales rep hold a conference call with the assigned writer to provide background info on the account.

6. The writer conducts a phone or on-site interview with the customer.

7. The first draft is submitted to the PR department, industry manager and sales rep. Collective comments are returned and edited. No other management team member is part of the editing process (poor use of their time).

8. The revised draft is then sent to the customer for approval.

9. Approved copy is formatted and printed, used first for public relations purposes (such as placing with a target vertical magazine), then used in various marketing communications materials.

Following these steps ensures that the focus is on the customer relationship and preserving goodwill. A single point of contact ensures that the customer does not receive a barrage of irritating requests. The form's intent is to establish expectations up front with the customer and to avoid surprises.

The emphasis throughout the project is on process rather than a case study "formula," to ensure quality, not quantity. Too many executives feel that case studies should follow a rigid consistent format, but since every customer application is unique, the format should be fluid enough to accommodate uniqueness and avoid boredom. And finally, limiting internal copy review to just the PR director and sales/industry managers helps streamline the process and eliminate conflicting agendas.

The following is a sample signoff form to email or fax to the customer before proceeding with the interview.

CUSTOMER SIGNOFF FORM

Dear Customer:

Sample Company values its relationships with its customers, and from time to time publishes brief case studies that summarize how its software is being applied in the customer's environment. These help the media and other customers to better understand the variety of our applications in various vertical markets.

We would like to obtain permission from you and your corporate representatives to assign a writer to interview you regarding your Sample Company experience. The writer will conduct the interview either at your company location or by telephone.

All of our case studies include the following components:

- An explanation of how our software/service is helping organizations improve their (business performance, sales, etc.)
- Quantifiable results if possible
- Graphics to illustrate the story, ranging from headshots to screenshots—these photos can be supplied by the customer or produced by Sample Company

The case study will not be used until it has obtained the appropriate signoff at your company. When approved, it may be used in several Sample Company marketing vehicles, including:

- Website
- Press release
- PowerPoint presentation
- Brochures
- Newsletters

Please indicate your permission for Sample Company to proceed with the interview by signing below and faxing it back to Dynamo PR Director, at 480-551-xxxx.

_____   _____

Authorized Customer Representative   Date

Feature Articles

One of the ongoing debates regarding articles is whether they should be written first and then placed, or placed first and then written to the magazine's specifications. The answer is that both approaches work.

To find opportunities and topics, it is necessary to review the published editorial calendars of each of your target magazines. These are generally available every fall for the following calendar year. Most people know to submit queries to editors several months before the issue date. But many companies don't know how to determine what data or information is publishable. What kinds of articles would other professionals in the vertical market want to read? This is where you should trust your PR director's research into the publications and his/her ongoing relationship with the various editors, rather than trying to jump in from an outside perspective. If you feel you simply *must* get a particular point across to your customers and prospects, consider a brochure or an advertisement, which are targeted directly to the end user and therefore easier to control.

The toughest part of producing articles these days is obtaining good photos and graphics. Your PR budget should include a line item for the creation of these graphics and for photo shoots. They will help tell the story and will significantly increase the chances of it being accepted. I have found it most helpful to use outside resources when creating graphics for a story—the outside creative person is motivated and brings a fresh perspective. Too many times, the inside marketing or technical person is too close to the story and wants to use PowerPoints as the supporting graphics. (Ugh! You wouldn't want to illustrate your wedding with PowerPoints, would you?)

Another challenge is extracting the information from the heads of the subject matter experts (SMEs) and conveying that on paper. They'll never have time to write the paper, so the fastest way to connect the dots is to interview them on the topic, tape the interview, transcribe it, and write a first draft. This gets them 80% of the way there. All the SME has to do is tweak the last 20%, and you're off to the editors. The interviewees can't argue with the content; after all, it's their own words against them!

White Papers

White papers are most helpful as public relations vehicles when they are educational and avoid being too "salesy." Readers know and understand that white papers are PR tactics, but are offended when they download a paper in the hopes of really finding something informative and instead are treated to two paragraphs of fluff explanation and then a series of blatant product promotions.

Used correctly, white papers can advance your company's image and position it as a leader in its market and a knowledgeable player in its category. They can double as a sales tool as well for prospects who find a research-based format informative. Here are some sample white paper topics, to distinguish from brochures or articles:

- Making the Business Case: Increasing Profitability in the Food and Beverage Industry

- Optimize Newspaper Circulation Revenues Through Customer Interaction Management Technology

- The Value and ROI of .Net Development

- A Strategy of Time: How Valuable Knowledge Gained Through the Y2K Effort Should be Preserved for Use in Future Projects

To enhance your white paper, have a clear industry issue or thesis that you are grappling with (take a look at your target publications' editorial calendars, and you'll see certain topics pop up again and again). Then, conduct a survey of your customers for real-world data to include, and research as much objective, third-party data as you can. Finally, it helps to format the white paper so that it looks like an academic paper as opposed to a glossy brochure, to convey a sense of timeliness, and not one of sales tactics.

Chapter 14:

Understanding Blogs, Podcasts, RSS Feeds and Wikis

"My blog, www.BobParsons.com, and my podcast, www.LifeOnline.com, give me direct contact with the public. I don't need to construct a news release to get my message out and I don't have to worry about my story being twisted. I started using this strategy with my blog before Go Daddy's first Super Bowl commercial aired and it has been quite effective. In today's fast-paced world of information overload, most boring news releases end up in the trash can!"
—Bob Parsons, CEO, the Go Daddy Group, Inc.

Blogs? Podcasting? RSS feeds? Wikis?

Do you feel as if the PR vocabulary around you is changing? Well, it is, but there's no need to panic. Just as typewriters gave way to VDTs to laptops to handheld digitals, the "equipment" of the PR profession is evolving, too, and some of the more recent developments require only an open mind and the willingness to spend some time learning about them in case you want to start putting them to use.

Ready? Sue MacDonald, a senior analyst at Nielsen Buzz-Metrics, has compiled the following overview of some of the most important new media in PR today:

Blogs

A blog is short for "web log," and it's an easily published website that serves as a source of opinion, information and online conversation, either by an individual or a group of like-minded "bloggers," the folks who write blogs. Is a blog like a website or a different animal altogether, you may ask? Frankly, it's a bit of both.

Blogs often look like web pages, but they have specific defining characteristics. A new entry published on a blog is called a "post," for example, and posts are usually displayed on the landing page (home page) in reverse chronological order, marked by date and time of day of publication. Most posts also have a permanent web URL, called a "permalink," and an author's profile that links to basic information about the author: name, locality, expertise/interests, contact information.

And while a corporate website requires content writers, technical support and a Webmaster, a blog requires only a free online blogging service (e.g., Blogger.com, LiveJournal, MySpace) or inexpensive blogging software (e.g., Movable Type, WordPress). It takes about 10 minutes to set it up (the blog services provide templates, content management tools and the ability to claim a blog title/URL as your own). Before you know it, you're the owner and author of your own blog, and you can add new content whenever and as often as you want.

What's unique about blogs? They've broken down the previous barriers that made websites expensive and time-consuming to publish and manage. Now, anyone with an opinion can blog about it. And because blog content is permanent, fresh and frequently updated, search engines find it easily. It usually works itself higher into search results more quickly than traditional (and more static) website copy.

What do bloggers write about? Everything and anything—politics, news events, products, services, hobbies, sports, children, travel, celebrities, media, entertainment, movies, music. You name it, there's a blogger covering the "beat."

Start your own blog: Can companies and brands launch their own blogs? Indeed. Blogs can link employees directly with customers. Blogs can open up customer conversations and interaction, feature upcoming industry developments, or give your company experts a platform for sharing information and their expertise with the world. Blogs can also be used for internal purposes only…for example, to serve as an employee communications tool, a place to post and share photos and documents, or a continuously updated company newsletter or forum.

Reach out to bloggers: Bloggers are important creators and spreaders of "news," and as such, PR professionals should consider reaching out to them with news tips, announcements and the like, just as they do to traditional media representatives. Just remember: bloggers write about what they're interested in, not what you think is important. Bloggers also consider themselves different from traditional media, yet even they rely heavily on mainstream news for commentary, reaction and yes, grandstanding. For optimum outreach, contact bloggers by e-mail, establish the relationship first, be transparent about your goals, and provide plenty of links and basic info when you invite them to write about you, your company or products, and your services.

Don't know where to start? Use some of the mainstream blog search engines, such as BlogPulse (www.blogpulse.com) or Technorati (www.technorati.com) to find out who's who and what's what in the blogosphere. Find blogs in your industry and begin building relationships.

Wiki

Another new online tool is called a "wiki," which is best thought of as a huge, interactive white board in cyberspace. Some say wiki is an acronym for "what I know is," but most agree its name comes from the "wiki wiki" line for buses at the Honolulu, Hawaii, airport ("wiki" means "fast" in Hawaiian). One of the most famous examples is the popular, multi-language online encyclopedia Wikipedia, (www.wikipedia.org). Like all wikis, it's a website whose users can add, remove, edit, or change content quickly and easily (including the ability to edit other contributors' additions; the wiki log keeps track of who made changes and when).

How can wikis be used? If you're in a company where numerous people need to edit, approve, and sign off on press releases, use the wiki as a central place where the release can be posted for review and where all authorized parties can edit it freely. Wikis are also used for project collaboration, internal communications, and shared information.

Some wikis can be created through online wiki providers, while others require special wiki software. The New PR Wiki (http://www.newprwiki.com) has plenty of information for the PR community.

Podcasts, Videocasts, Streaming Video

PR is no longer just about words. It's about images, voices, movies, and various other new media, all of which can now be created and shared on common devices such as cell phone cameras, digital cameras, iPods, MP3 players and other handheld digital devices.

Podcasting refers to a collection of technologies that allow audio and video recordings to be distributed and shared over the internet. Instead of turning on a radio or TV to listen to and watch signals beamed through the air, audio and video programs can be turned into files that are stored on computer servers, linked to on

websites, downloaded by users who visit those websites and lis-
tened to and watched immediately (or saved for later) on devices
such as iPods and MP3 players. And the files are almost always free
or incredibly low-cost.

How can PR pros use podcasting? Make your press releases,
investor updates, and analyst briefings available on your website in
text and audio/video format (or all three). Provide audio/video
versions of new product announcements, "how-to" videos or
troubleshooting demonstrations on your website for customers,
partners, repair professionals, and retail outlets.

Record your latest advertising jingle as a downloadable
podcast, or make a 30-second commercial available as a viewable
download that your website visitors can share with others. Turn
internal newsletters/employee announcements into podcasts for
employees (especially those in remote locations).

RSS Feeds

It used to be that a news editor at a media outlet (newspaper,
TV newsroom, radio station, magazine) read through hundreds of
articles sent daily over syndicated news wires and decided which
departments got which stories: hard news to the news desk, sports
stories to the sports desk, entertainment and celebrity news to the
lifestyle section, opinion pieces to the editorial page, business news
to the business section, etc.

Today, internet users get to set up their own versions of these
wire desks by subscribing to RSS feeds that are embedded into
online content. RSS stands for Really Simple Syndication, and it's
a way that internet users can have relevant information and news
delivered directly to them instead of having to surf through hundreds of news sources each day hoping to find what's relevant.

If you've ever set up a Google News alert based on a certain
keyword, company name or brand name, you've used an RSS feed
without knowing the technology behind it.

Entire services have built up around the RSS phenomenon, including companies such as Feed Demon, NetNewswire and others that will compile and organize RSS feeds into your e-mail system. There are also online services that aggregate RSS feeds for you, such as MyYahoo, BlogLines and NewsGator (some newer computer operating systems have RSS functions already built in).

RSS in action: Set up RSS feeds for particular topics, issues, trends, companies, brand names or competitors to keep yourself updated in real time; alerts will either be sent directly to your e-mail box or stored for you in the aggregator you've chosen. Likewise, consider embedding RSS feeds on your own website or blog to make sure others can receive timely updates from you.

For the technologically challenged/fearful: If you're ever clueless or filled with trepidation about new technologies, devices, equipment or Internet trends, here's a tip that always works: hire a tech-savvy high school kid or college intern for a few months, tell them what you need, and turn them loose. Be sure to ask as many questions as you can, and you'll learn as much from them as they do from you!

Chapter 15:

Don't Neglect Media Training

---

*"When you hear a particularly good media or analyst inter-
view with one of your peers, chances are he or she has had
media training. Speaking off the cuff with the media, assuming the talent will hit you like a lightning bolt when the time
comes, is the second biggest mistake you can make. Saying 'no
comment' to a reporter is the biggest."*
— Roy Heffley, Media Trainer,
Bob Moomey Communications

Media training should be on your list of to-dos, regardless of
whether it has been conducted before at your company site. There
are two areas of focus in order to be effective with the media: content and delivery. Some executives excel at content—they know a
lot about the product or the market—but have trouble with the
delivery of the information.

I remember working with one executive who had an interview scheduled at a financial news radio station. He was to talk
about his company, so he wrote his entire Q&A session on index
cards, which he proceeded to line up neatly on the counter when

we arrived at the station. When the interviewer asked questions out of order, however, the executive was completely taken aback, and wasted time while he frantically searched his note cards. Listening to the tape of the interview, you hear a lot of long pauses after the questions were asked, during which the executive was searching for his written crutches.

Other management types are wonderful presenters, but never seem to answer the question at hand. They spend a lot of time talking about themselves or trying to impress the editor or analyst, but fail to directly address the question. During one teleconference I attended, the analyst, who was on the phone in another state, cut off the executive mid-sentence and quickly wrapped up the call.

In another face-to-face press visit, an executive launched the meeting with, "Let me tell you about Company ABC." The editor, a brusque New Englander, put her hand up immediately to stop him, and replied, "Please don't. Just tell me who your customers are. All I want to know is, do you have any good case studies?"

Media training is a good idea for two reasons: 1) It prepares you for the unexpected, such as a crisis or market trend that impacts your business, and 2) It helps you hone your company message for impatient editors and analysts.

The best media trainers are those who have spent some time in broadcasting, where they've learned the "60 Minutes" type questioning that can make anyone's knees buckle. "Is it true that your product killed thousands in India?"

Based on her earlier media training, Jefferson Wells executive Julie McCollum learned how to stay focused on mutually agreed upon objectives. When she was hired to open an office in the southwest, a local reporter requested an interview. Expecting questions about the history of the new firm and related plans for expansion and growth, she was surprised to find that the reporter instead asked questions about her previous company.

Fortunately, McCollum's media training had taught her how to deal with unexpected questions in a non-defensive and non-controversial manner, and how to re-direct the focus to the topic that was agreed upon when the original interview was set up.

It's easy when speaking to the press to be lulled into a comfort level that makes you believe what you say is off the record. It isn't. Treat all your discourse as official. It's also tempting to say, "No comment," just like they do in the movies. Stonewalling doesn't work, however. It helps to be trained by a professional who can guide you through practice questions and answers so that two-way communication is facilitated with your target audiences.

I was lucky enough to be exposed to public speaking through a course in graduate school, active participation in a Denver Toastmasters chapter, and a one-day course in media training at a corporate site. Until you have seen yourself video-taped, you have no idea of your idiosyncratic gestures and deer-in-the-headlight stares. It's a wonderful, humbling experience.

Those who truly understand the media know that it's not a one-stop deal; rather, it's something you have to keep doing, like mowing the grass! In this instance, the adage of "A job well done need never be done again" does not apply. If management claims they don't need media training, it's because they fear looking foolish in front of their peers. Better to look foolish now, however, than when the local TV station is outside your door or when the key analyst for your market asks a difficult question.

Chapter 16:

The Essentials of Effective Press Tours and Press Conferences

---

"The most effective briefings are those in which firms come in with important news and a prepared message. This almost always leads to written coverage. To maximize the value for your company in these briefings, recognize that analysts (as well as editors) have a lot of competitive insight because they are hearing everyone's story and talking to customers. Don't discount this by not caring about their input, questions, and feedback."

—Tony Friscia, President and CEO, AMR Research

Press tours and conferences aren't used as much as they were several years ago, with the advent of electronic communication, increased airport security, popularity of webcasts, and other factors that have made travel less desirable to vendor companies and media alike. Conducted judiciously, however, press tours and conferences can be extremely effective, as there is nothing quite like personal face-to-face communication.

Press Tours

One-on-one meetings with editors and analysts are effective if your company has a new executive to introduce to the market, a significant product development, a merger/acquisition, or a significant shift in market strategy. Your entourage should include an experienced spokesperson/expert on the topic to be addressed, and the PR director. Two or three company employees maximum are ideal; any more than that and you overwhelm the editor or analyst with whom you're meeting.

Generally, the tours identify two to three key cities that have a cluster of media, typically Boston, NYC, Chicago and San Francisco. Most executives have been on press tours and claim to be "old hats" at it; yet, here are some of the common missteps I've seen during press visits:

1. The executive is still so new to the company that he or she can't yet speak intelligently about the market—like an onion that is quite bare after the first layer of knowledge is peeled back.

2. The executive hasn't been coached (or hasn't heeded advice) on how to briefly explain the announcement and then wait patiently for the media to ask questions.

3. The spokesperson wasn't coached on (or didn't do his/her homework on) the background of the editor/analyst to be met, resulting in the spokesperson knowing nothing about the publication or analyst group, calling the editor by the wrong name, and/or confusing the publication with a similar-sounding magazine. One executive, for example, met with Control Magazine but confused it with Control Engineering Magazine. Yes, both magazines are headquartered in Illinois, but obviously have different editorial staff and different editorial objectives.

4. Not enough time is allotted between visits, so the tour team is rushing from one site to another. It's advisable to limit the number of daily visits to three or four to keep things sane.

5. Detailed, written directions from one publication to another were not obtained sufficiently ahead of time. One company hired a limousine driver who *thought* he knew where they were headed, but ended up taking them 15 minutes in the wrong direction in plodding Boston traffic. They arrived at the magazine's office late and harried.

6. Economy hotels and non-direct flights were chosen at the expense of the tour team's arriving well-rested and comfortable. This may seem prima donna-like and irresponsible in this day and age of corporate budget downsizing, but if you are going to take the time to meet with the editors on their turf, do everything possible to arrive fresh and ready to be "on."

Press Conferences

You should hold a press conference only if you truly have news that warrants a special trip by the media. Examples might be a significant merger or acquisition, a revolutionary product launch (something that does cure cancer, not the latest version of your software), or a new CEO.

At one company I worked with, there was a significant announcement in the mid '90s regarding collaborative efforts to solve a challenging industry problem at the time—Y2K. As many of the target media were located in Boston, we chose to conduct our press conference there to launch this collaborative effort. Much consideration went into the choice of location, date, and time for the event, after checking with the editors.

We decided on a program that had check-in from 11:30 – 11:45 a.m., lunch served at 11:45, with presentations during lunch from 12:00 – 12:45 p.m., and Q&A from 12:45 – 1:00 p.m. The month chosen was January, which was admittedly risky in terms of possible snowfall, but also a quiet month travel-wise for editors, with few conflicts. The day of the week was Tuesday, to avoid end-of-week deadlines. It was held in downtown Boston at the Ritz Carlton, a hotel known for its top service and comparatively easy location right off the Mass Pike and Storrow Drive.

Parking was validated to save the media the hassle of having to pay high fees. Media guests could stay longer if they wanted to, but the event was designed to be brief and informative. Of 30 local media invited, 28 analysts and editors accepted and attended the event—a remarkable percentage.

For another large company with strong industry market share, but little local presence in its hometown, we arranged a press conference to announce a new training center they had built at headquarters. This was scheduled as a breakfast with the division president, with a shuttle bus (it was 105 degrees outside!) to cart the editors to the new building for a tour of the facilities. The only factor we hadn't anticipated during the course of the event was that some of the female reporters were wearing dresses, which made climbing up the steep steps into a shuttle van a little awkward. (It isn't always possible to think through every scenario!)

When arranging a press conference, it helps to prepare a checklist, send out invitations early, and conduct a dry run with the executives a day or two before the event. Do not let them wing it! The editors will know if the presentations and schedule are conducted in a seat-of-the-pants manner. And try to do something unusual to keep the format moving and interesting. How many dull commencement speeches or school plays have you attended? Everyone wants to learn something new and to be entertained.

Most important, everyone is on a hectic time schedule. Never assume that just because the topic is near and dear to your heart, media members will want to take a huge chunk out of their day to hear about it. You must have solid news value to make a press conference a viable tactic. If you can, poll your target media to learn the following preferences:

- Optimum day of the week
- Time of month
- Best location
- Breakfast or lunch format
- Whether they want a demo or "just the facts, ma'am"

Whenever you hold an event involving the media, it is perfectly acceptable to poll a few ahead of time to solicit feedback on how best to structure the event. Assuming you know what to include in a press tour or conference may result in tailoring the information incorrectly and unnecessarily alienating part of your target audience.

Chapter 17:

How to Have a Successful Product Launch

"The product launch must be an integral part of the develop ment process and not an afterthought when the software is complete. It is suicide to wait until the product is ready before engaging the PR group, as this assumes it is a sequential process, rather than a collaborative one."
—Mark Wheeler, Senior Manager,
Corporate Automation Engineering, Genentech

I tend to wince when I receive calls from prospects who tell me, "Hey, we have just finished our new product, and we want to launch next week—can you help us?" They clearly think PR is just something you turn on automatically—just announce the product and its reputation will grow like a weed and sales will come pouring in. This again is the "sales support mentality," where PR is used as a reactive isolated communication tool as opposed to a strategic one.

Unless you've first tended to your target media audience carefully and primed it for the launch, you're wasting your time, not to mention the money and effort behind the press release. Here's how to make the best of your product launches:

1. Meet with your research and development team to determine the approximate rollout time of the product, and when it will be sent to identified beta sites. Schedule the formal PR launch to occur about two weeks after the estimated availability time, in case there are the inevitable delays.

2. Set up teleconferences or webcasts with a few key industry analysts approximately four weeks before the official launch. (If possible, conduct the teleconferences even earlier to solicit input and direction from the analysts on what should be included in the product before it's even designed). But if you didn't have this foresight, at least notify them about a month before the announcement officially goes out. This ensures that they are well-versed in the product's features so that they can speak intelligently about your product, and serve as a possible resource for editors who have questions.

3. If possible, send them a web link to a demo version of the product or service.

4. Take their input to heart regarding how to shape the messaging.

5. Consider overnight shipping copies of your product to a "top 10" list of media a full week prior to the event.

6. Prepare a Q&A on the product, either for internal use (to explore potentially dangerous questions that might be asked) and/or for external use (standard information such as pricing, availability, strengths vs. competition weaknesses, etc).

7. Integrate the timing of the press release with your other marketing communication vehicles as part of a combined launch—advertising, website, direct mail, e-blasts, webcasts,

trade shows, customer letters, and so on. Do not rely solely on a press release to launch your product!

8. Set up press visits with a few key media in person in advance of the formal launch.

9. Prepare a few items to have on hand to send to selective editors on the launch date, including names of beta customers willing to speak to the press, and screen shots (or other appropriate graphics) in various formats.

I've noticed that the most successful launches involve a product that had the right idea, the right market, and the right presentation. By "presentation" I'm referring to the way in which the product was explained and unveiled to the market. Successful launches include the analysts up front for valuable input, deliver complete information to the editors, and provide it in an interesting and novel way.

We solicited the input of a prominent e-learning industry analyst when announcing a new training product that was available on a PDA (Personal Digital Assistant) for the first time. The analyst suggested that we load the training software up on the PDAs and express ship them on a loaner basis to key editors and analysts. The shipment included instructions on how to use the PDA, the length of time the recipient could demo it until it had to be returned (in enclosed pre-paid return shipping envelopes) and background information on why the training was unique and how it was specifically developed for this new medium. The results were extremely positive for the product and the company. This is testament to good planning as well as to the benefits of seeking outside input early on when promoting products or services.

For the launch of a new platform-independent batch software product in the mid '90s, we first contacted several industry analysts to obtain their comments on the significance of the announcement to the industry. Their feedback became part of the general press information made available on launch day, to show that the product wasn't just "vaporware" but had actually been examined by some analysts. We chose a key annual industry trade show at which to launch the software, and held a special press conference complete with tuxedo-clad executives. The press conference featured a new multimedia presentation about the product at a time when multimedia was still in its infancy and a new concept for editors and analysts.

We also made sure that the traditional press kits in the press room were enclosed in a special "press kit tower" that stood apart from the other kits in the room and made it easy for media to locate the company's information.

All of these factors took several months of planning, and would not have been possible had the development team not been in close cooperation with the marketing group, keeping them apprised of the product's development schedule. The importance of such collaboration and communication cannot be over-emphasized.

Chapter 18:

Webcasts, Open Houses, Surveys and Awards

"Today, it is critical to have numerous touch points with customers—both current and potential—across three areas: in print, in person, and online. This three-sided approach to communications is so vital today because of the varied ways in which people absorb information in a time when they are continuously bombarded with messages."
—David Greenfield, Publisher,
Manufacturing Business Technology magazine

Most people think of press releases when they think of PR, but that is like thinking that working for an airline can only mean you're a flight attendant. There are so many other integral responsibilities that are included in the total airline business—ground crew, maintenance crew, pilots, food staff, registration, travel agents, etc. Flight attendants may be the most *visible* aspect to you when you take a plane trip, but everything works together to create a successful experience.

Similarly, a viable PR program operates under the knowledge that it will require many different types of deliverables to promote the company image and awareness. These run the gamut of webcasts, books, executive guides (like this one), open houses, surveys, and awards, to name just a few.

Webcasts

Webcasts are often used to communicate an important message to a broad range of audience. They are very economical and most are very informative and entertaining, having come a long way from the dry presentations of the late 90s. When preparing a webcast for your company, there are numerous aspects to consider. It helps to have a dedicated team for these events, so that their knowledge is learned and repeatable. Following is a checklist you can use for planning a webcast to announce your next product release or partnership.

Pre-Planning

Identify customer/executive to be featured speaker	
Determine date and best time of day	
Identify topic	
Reserve studio or sound-proof room	
Line up telecommunications	
Line up audio talent	
Set up hotel/flights for customer if they plan to be on-site for the webcast	

Promotion/Publicity

Discuss joint promotion with customer, including use of mailing lists, website, direct mail, special events, etc.	
Prepare draft copy for web and other promotional efforts	
Create the copy and invitation for customers	
Obtain a photo of the presenter	
Send early notification to the sales team	
Prepare the sales teams and employees on positioning, including how and what to promote to their customers and prospects	
Remind the sales team and employees to access the webcast (if there are enough "seats")	
Create an online support area for the event	
Notify editors and analysts	
Notify customers and prospects	

Preparation

Prepare a one-page audio/PC tip sheet and/or FAQ (frequently asked questions) for customers	
Conduct a run through with just the customer the week prior to event, by phone	
Conduct a dress rehearsal/walk through one day before the event	
Send a link of previous webcasts as an example	
Obtain bio of the presenter	

Presentation

Create content	
Hold an initial teleconference to discuss/walk through the presentation, prior to the audio dress rehearsal	
Include pictures of speakers in the opening slide of the presentation so attendees know who is talking	
Proofread the presentation	
Upload to a web-based platform	

Host Preparation

Prepare a script for the introduction of the webcast and the presenter	
Prepare questions for the host to ask the presenter	

Registration/Logistics

Create a registration form and post it on the web site	
Log in the registrations alphabetically by the company name	
Create a follow-up e-mail to send registrants a few days prior to the event	

Miscellaneous

Identify any prearranged questions from the audience	
Ensure the audio talent has information to introduce the speakers	

Follow-up/Archiving

Finalize the registration list	
Total up telecommunication costs	
After the event, prepare a Flash presentation with audio to include on the website	
Prepare any necessary, brief web copy to accompany the presentation for its archived postings to the website	
Post the presentation on the web	
Prepare and send a follow-up e-mail and web link to attendees	

Open House

For local goodwill, as well as employee goodwill, nothing beats an open house. Occasions for such an event might be a new building, an expanded building, anniversary, or a new location. Before you plan your event, determine your primary objective. Do you want to promote the company as a role model? Do you want to show the company's strong growth in a particular area? Do you want to showcase a unique product or approach?

One company wanted to demonstrate how its e-learning was conducted in live studios on-site, which had glass panels through which visitors could watch the instructors "training" an unseen audience. Another company held an open house to showcase its larger headquarters facility just to employees and their families.

Once you know your objective, determine your audience. Attendees can include local customers, print media, politicians and dignitaries, broadcast media, economic development organizations, business groups, and chambers of commerce. If appropriate and possible, you might have a celebrity on hand to help add to the excitement of the open house, such as a civic leader, sports figure, prominent author, etc.

There are many books written on the subject of events, but from a PR perspective, an open house might involve a donation to a local charity, a raffle, and/or a ribbon cutting. Most open houses also include formal remarks from the appropriate executive, a tour of the new or expanded facility, giveaway items, and hors d'oeuvres and beverages. You might also have on hand small press kits for the media, although kits are on the way out in favor of electronic communication these days. And don't forget a photographer if you want to include photos on your website and in the company newsletter.

Surveys

Surveys need not always be conducted by an expensive outside firm, although that route certainly provides a high level of credibility and objectivity. There is also value in conducting your own internal surveys of your customers. No one else will have access to this dataset, so you might as well leverage it. Examples of areas you can survey include feedback on training classes or new products, status of progress in compliancy on an industry regulation, opinions on a particular issue in the industry, and so on. If you poll your customers and summarize the information objectively and in pie chart form, most editors and analysts will use this information. It represents one more valuable data point to round out the perspective on any given issue in the market.

The costs of surveys can sometimes be prohibitive. You might consider co-branding the survey with like-minded organizations and associations, or in some cases, the magazines themselves. Co-branding not only enhances credibility but spreads the costs among multiple parties.

Once you've completed the survey and analysis, you can use the results in the form of a press release, or submit as an exclusive to a magazine. The former is probably the best route, as you can then promote the information to as wide a range of media as possible.

Awards

Awards are a valuable PR tactic because they not only help you create a positive image of the company, but you end up with re-usable copy describing the organization. Most award forms are fairly standard, requiring consistent information about your company's mission, product lines, differentiators, financials (under NDA), partnerships, and key customers. Once you've created one complete form, you can use it for other award submissions by merely tweaking the copy. There are often modest fees associated with the submissions as well, so it's good to have a line item in the PR budget dedicated to such fees.

The key to winning awards is pretty simple—you can't win if you don't play. Many award competitions have few entries, so your chances of winning are greatly increased if you actually enter and do so within the deadline and with a complete, detailed form that follows the requirements to a "T."

Style is important when submitting award copy. You want to be informative and straightforward, yet convey the uniqueness and excitement of the company or product, as well. Think of 10K copy that's ratcheted up a notch!

If you have someone on your sales team who is responsible for overseeing RFP (request for proposal) or other sales proposals, he or she may already have some descriptive copy about the company that you can use. Just remember not to boldly claim that your company or product is "the best" in the award copy, unless you can back it up with substantiating data from an analyst firm. You need to present the facts as they are, and let the judging team reach the conclusion that you're the best. If you steal their evaluative thunder by proclaiming victory too early, they'll be too tempted to bring you down a peg or two.

Chapter 19:

Speaking of Speaking

"The key difference between a good presentation and a GREAT presentation is passion. Knowing your material is mandatory. Knowing your audience is essential. But delivering your message with passion is what makes the presentation memorable."
—Michael Saucier, CEO, Transpara, Inc.

What is your greatest fear? Flying? Snakes? Deep-sea diving?

If you're like many people, public speaking ranks very high on your list of phobias. There is something about having to stand up in front of an audience and deliver information—while being entertaining at the same time—that seems to make even the most courageous business person falter.

In general, there are two kinds of speaking opportunities: those targeted to your particular industry, and those targeted to your local community. Both represent value to your business in terms of image, goodwill, recognition, and possible future business down the road.

Number one on your "to-do" list to get ready for speaking opportunities should be to practice this skill.

Get Practice

There is no shortcut to overriding the fear of public speaking. It's a lot like swimming: to learn best, you have to jump right in.

Without delay, if you haven't had training in public speaking before, research the possibilities available in your town and choose the best one for you. Some examples are joining Toastmasters (www.toastmasters.org), a civic organization that meets weekly and offers you the opportunity to test your speaking skills in a variety of formats; signing up for a Dale Carnegie public speaking workshop (www.dalecarnegietraining.com); or taking a public speaking course at the local community college.

What to Do When You're Asked to Speak

If you're invited to present at a trade show, conference, or local community event, by all means say, "Yes!" It means more practice and more visibility for your business, as well as for your leadership within that industry. Here are some points to remember, to ensure the event goes well:

- **Know what you're walking into:** Find out ahead of time from the event coordinator how big the room will be, what equipment will be available, what the dress code will be, how many attendees are expected, and where you are in the program—are you at the beginning? The middle? The end? Will you be allowed and/or expected to have handouts available? Knowing this information helps you prepare your presentation.

■ **Know your audience ahead of time:** Find out from the event organizer the top two or three issues that keep the audience up at night, and reference those in your presentation. This helps you come across as someone who is familiar with their situation, and not just reading from a canned speech that you've delivered dozens of times. I've heard the same speaker present at different industry conferences with absolutely no change in the content or delivery, and with nothing in the material that referenced the particular audience in the room.

■ **Do not read from notes:** This is where Toastmasters and seminars that focus on public speaking can help wean you from the comfort of notes to the power of seemingly extemporaneous presentations. Reading from prepared notes may make you feel safe, but it results in a very dry presentation and gives the audience the impression that you don't really know your subject matter, else why would you need "cheat sheets?" Only the President can get away with this—and he usually has a teleprompter! Unless you have the capability to write as eloquently as the Gettysburg Address, don't bring anything more than perhaps 1-2 note cards to jog your memory.

■ **Use graphics, an overhead projector or video only if you are adept at handling them** (or if you have someone from your staff who can run them capably): While graphics are great support for a presentation, they need to run smoothly. If you are not comfortable running the equipment or speaking to graphics behind you without having to constantly turn around to read the bullet points or other information, stick to just the podium speech and leave the graphics out. It will be too disconcerting otherwise for your audience.

- **Bring two other people from your company:** They can handle the projector and manage the handouts or any other emergencies that crop up. It is inevitable that there will be some last minute flurry of tasks that need attention, and you don't want to have your concentration diverted. It's advisable to have support staff to help you out.

- **Find out how much time you'll have:** Know how long the event coordinator wants you to present for, and don't go over the limit! Wear a watch and put it on the podium, if there is one. Or agree ahead of time on a signal with one of your staff to indicate when you have only five minutes left. They can stand in the back of the room and raise their hand, scratch their head, whatever you agree on.

- **Publicize the event on your website:** Here is a golden opportunity to promote your speaking opportunity beyond the actual event itself. Start building an area on your business website for news and events.

How to Find Speaking Opportunities

Once you gain a level of comfort speaking, find places to present that will benefit you, your company and your industry. Most speaking opportunities are lined up anywhere from a few months to two years prior to the event. It's rare that you'll be asked to fill a slot at the 11th hour, or that you'll be able to land a speaking slot at that late date. So the best advice is to be prepared. Here are some ways to unearth opportunities:

- The more people who know you, the more who'll think of you when they need speakers: join trade associations and local chambers of commerce. Visibility = mindshare = speaking opportunities.

- Within the organization to which you belong, volunteer for a position that will give you a chance to make presentations or to lead a committee.

- Contact trade associations for information on their conferences at least *one year* prior to the conference date. Be ready to submit an abstract and biography.

- Volunteer to speak. You can start small, with local organizations. In this way, you build your speaking resume. Many trade associations, along with a request for your abstract, ask for a list of conferences or meetings at which you've presented.

What Every Speaker Should Have

There are three things that every speaker should have on hand and kept updated at all times: a good digital or traditional color head-and-shoulders corporate photo, taken by a good photographer—please, no cheap photos taken against your company wall!; a brief bio; and a brief abstract of what the presentation will be about. See samples below of a standard bio and paper abstract:

Bio:

John Doe is the owner of Doe Masonry, a Cary, North Carolina-based company specializing in building with stone and rock. He has more than 30 years of experience in masonry and stonemasonry. Doe previously served as president of Jones Limestone and was regional vice-president of the Mason Contractors Association of America (MCAA). Doe has a bachelor's degree in Civil Engineering and is the author of several technical papers on stone masonry presented at MCAA conferences, as well as articles published in *Masonry Magazine*. He has also presented at several industry conferences.

Abstract:

"Leave no stone unturned." Dimensional stone is an old building material making a comeback in the U.S. As more architects design for this material, more masons need to explore its fine points and develop strategies for constructing the buildings those architects will create. This paper will define the market, the material and the masonry methods best suited for creating stone buildings of beauty and durability.

Once you have these three elements, a bio, photo and abstract of the presentation, the rest is easy. Just practice, practice, practice and more practice.

Chapter 20:

Goodwill Hunting—Community Activities Are Good PR

"If organizations become involved within the communities in which they work, play, and live, they will receive a return far greater than what they ever thought possible. The return will come from feeling good about their organization, team building, goodwill, and a sense of belonging. The net effect to the bottom line is that an organization involved with the community will be included in business transactions they never thought possible!"
—Tim Moman, CEO, Edgepoint Technology

There's a famous saying that no good deed ever goes unpunished, but in the case of public relations, it's perhaps more accurate to say that no good deed should ever go unpublicized.

For example, since many mason contractors are involved in community efforts such as donating their talent to Habitat for Humanity, restoring public monuments, rebuilding historic sites and the like, it makes sense for them to "get the word out."

Companies forget to promote their community-oriented activities for a variety of reasons. Some are too preoccupied with marketing their corporate products to their customers, while others are primarily focused on meeting quarterly financial goals. Another group feels reluctant to talk about their charitable actions publicly, thinking that it might come across as too self-serving.

There is a straightforward approach to getting the word out to the media about your company, however, without appearing to be opportunistic. The media appreciates good, solid information and there are appropriate ways and means to communicate all of your business activities to them, including the ones that fall into the "goodwill" category.

The following are seven major steps to identifying and communicating your charitable activities in a tasteful manner:

- **Designate one person in the company to be your community relations archivist**—It's important (and will create fewer headaches later) if you decide that one person in your company will serve as the compiler and clearinghouse for all information related to your business' community or charitable activities. This person can be from any department, but is often found in Public Relations or Human Resources. In a family-owned business, the owner or owner's spouse usually shoulders this burden until "the kids" are old enough.

- **Poll your employees**—Once designated, your point person should conduct a simple poll of your employees, whether you have two or 200, to find out the non-profit organizations or charities in which they actively participate, either as volunteer or board of directors members. Examples might be Big Brothers/Big Sisters, the American Cancer Society, Habitat for Humanity, or Toys for Tots. Compile this information and look for any common themes.

■ **Get as much information on the charity or recipient as you can**—When providing information to the press, keep in mind that the goal is to talk about the recipient(s) of your efforts, not so much about your company. The PR value comes in being attached to a charity through your laudable efforts. If the charity has a website, pull a summary description from it to keep in your files. If they have a public relations manager, contact him or her and ask for a corporate backgrounder. As you're compiling information, you want to be able to provide the reporter with a succinct summary of what the charitable organization is all about. And make sure you let the charity know that you intend to send information to the press. They might be able to expand your media list with a media database of their own.

■ **Find the stats**—Figures and data make for interesting copy. One company, for example, asked its employees to donate to the Marine's Toys for Tots program. In just three days, over 500 toys were collected, an admirable number for a company that had only 200 employees. The Toys for Tots program was able to say that this exceeded typical company donations and provided data on how many toys it had received to date. You want to include this kind of data in your information to reporters because it puts your contribution in context.

■ **Update your media database**—If you haven't already, make sure you have a good, qualified list of local and regional media in your database. Don't forget: information about your goodwill activities is interesting both to local media and to trade media as well—i.e., the magazines that are dedicated to your industry.

■ **Send the information as an editorial alert, not as a press release**—There are many ways of sending information to reporters. Most people automatically think of press releases, but these represent the most formal (and usually most abused) method for disseminating information. Another more appropriate form for communicating your community activities is the so-called "media alert" or "editorial alert." In this approach, you email 1-2 brief summary paragraphs to appropriate editors to let them know about your activity. It's up to them whether or not they publish it, but you get the point across without grandstanding.

Let's take a look at how you can develop this type of "info-mercial." The subject line could be "Editorial Alert: Acme Masonry Collects 500 Toys for Tots in Time for Holiday." The information in the body of the email would contain factual, non-promotional information, including how and why Acme collected the toys, why the number 500 is significant (i.e., most companies only submit 50-60 toys), and background information on the Toys for Tots organization.

Here's an example:

Acme Masonry recently collected more than 500 toys from its 200 employees as part of its annual holiday participation in the U.S. Marine Corps Reserve Toys for Tots program. According to HR Manager Sally Field, the room at Acme set aside for the toys was filled in just 3 days. The U.S. Marine Corps Reserve Toys for Tots Program is the Marine Corps' premier community action program and the only charitable endeavor within the Department of Defense that reaches outside the military. It gives something back to the communities from which the nation draws the young men and women who wear the uniforms of the armed services of the United States. According to the program's leader, the 500 toys represent a record-breaking number for a company of Acme's size. For more information on the program, visit www.toysfortots.org.

- **Be selective in what you publicize**—If your company is very active through its corporate or individual employee efforts, have your community relations point person analyze the activities and determine trends. You could send out an editorial alert, for example, that promotes all activities in the company associated with the American Cancer Society or American Heart Association, or all activities that have to do with local housing projects, and so on. But be selective. You shouldn't be sending out alerts any more frequently than three times a year.

Don't make the media go hunting for your goodwill. Let them hear about it, and give them the facts they need. It's a win-win situation for you, the reporter, and the charity with which you're working.

Chapter 21:

Trade Shows and PR Support

"Trade shows and conferences offer an excellent opportunity to reach many targets. One critical target is the media and analysts—two key influencers for trade show and conference attendees. No company should expect to achieve full ROI from a trade show or conference unless a fully integrated marketing communications plan includes public relations."
—Rozanne Bonavito, Director of Marketing
Communications, Pillar Data Systems

While trade shows and industry conferences are perfect venues for your target customers and prospects, they are usually attended as well by key media for that market, or at minimum, by the sponsoring publication for the event.

Over the years, PR support for trade shows has evolved to keep up with the times. The thick, hardcopy press kits of yesterday have now been replaced by online services to which you submit your announcement ahead of the event. Editors don't have to lug the numerous kits around anymore, a fact for which they are eternally grateful. I still remember seeing editors gut kit after kit at trade shows, leaving behind a press room full of covers, slides, and other useless material, and taking only the precious few announcements that they felt amounted to anything.

If you are planning a PR announcement in tandem with a trade show, keep several factors in mind. There will be competing announcements from other companies at the show. If you have a small company, consider pre-announcing a week before the event, rather than at the show. This gives you a head start over your larger competitors, who no doubt will have the largest booth space and the largest mindshare of the media.

Remember, too, that members of the press have dozens of companies to cover when they report on a show. While you have the advantage of standing in one location all the time, they must traverse the show floor while enduring boring company spokespersons and having to assimilate different product information in a short time. Unless your company has significant market share in your industry, consider conducting your press announcement at a separate time.

If you feel, however, that your organization is of sufficient size and the announcement of sufficient value that PR activity at the show is preferred, tailor the information appropriately. You can have a few hardcopy kits on hand (sometimes the editors will take notes on the press releases themselves), but be sure to have a complete electronic version you can email to the editor.

If possible, have a variety of graphics available and give separate graphics to each major publication so they feel they have a unique product shot to include. Include a Q&A with the announcement. Ensure that your key spokesperson is at the booth at the appointed time. If possible, meet in a secluded area so that the reporter and spokesperson can be heard and can talk without interruption. And offer to overnight the hard copy to the reporter's business address if feasible.

When scheduling appointments with the media, contact them about 3-4 weeks prior to the show. Any earlier than that, and they won't have a good idea of how many companies they will be assigned to cover at the show. Any later than that, and you may end up the last company on their list.

There are also benefits to holding your major announcement at a smaller trade show, rather than the big annual event. My first assignment at Data General was to cover a small design automation conference in Albuquerque, while the more senior PR specialists held court at a separate corporate press launch in NYC. Although the corporate launch was attended by several of the key financial and business press, the New Mexico conference was a veritable fish hatchery of key vertical market media. As a result, I was able to schedule a record 26 interviews in 2.5 days. Now that I'm 47 instead of 24, I don't know if I have the energy to withstand that grueling appointment schedule, but at the time, it was thrilling. The conference garnered key coverage for Data General's product announcement, which was a technical workstation bundled with software. Sometimes the best way to get attention when it comes to trade shows is to avoid the obvious.

Chapter 22:

Be Aware of Legal Regulations

"In a world where anything that's said can be immediately published online and distributed to millions, and there are increasing regulations from privacy laws to Sarbanes-Oxley requiring rigorous compliance with corporate policy, it has never been more important for corporate executives to think before they speak. Executives need to work closely with their strategic public relations professionals, and seek their advice not just when disaster strikes but in advance of making any public statement."

—Steven Weinberg, Shareholder, Greenberg Traurig LLP

Did you know that marketing and PR materials are, in fact, legal documents? Any claims you make in them can and will be held against you. You will be able to avoid 99% of the legal ramifications of your PR activities if you follow just three simple steps:

1. Remember that every press announcement, speaking opportunity, webcast, or other public document or display becomes an archived "matter of record"—it sets the tone and precedent for the company and can be retrieved easily in this age of

electronics. Think of these activities and documents as legal actions and documents with long-term implications.

2. Anytime you are involved in an announcement that refers to another company and its products, or in an announcement or activity conducted jointly with another company, include their legal and PR departments on your approval list for copy. This protects you to some small degree because you can prove that you issued any formal announcements with their approval and knowledge. It also affords them an opportunity to correct any mistakes you have inadvertently made (such as omitting trademarks, or attributing superfluous and/or inaccurate quotes to that partnering company's executives).

3. Conduct all PR as if it were going to appear on the front page of the Wall Street Journal the next morning. Particularly with the advent of regulations such as Sarbanes-Oxley, it's important for a company's PR activities to stay on the right side of the law. Over the years, I've seen a few examples where overzealous tactics landed the PR professional or company in a hot spot. At one company, the marketing industry manager was calling on a well-known food manufacturing firm. The manager obtained a quote from one of the production line people and turned it into a mini case study. The case study was published, but unfortunately, the production line person did not have the authority to provide quotes to outside entities. Nor did the manufacturing company permit "testimonials" of this sort. The result was damaged credibility and lack of confidence in the software vendor for whom the marketing industry manager worked.

In another instance, a marketing executive wanted to issue a press release about his company's recent agreement with a large airline in the U.S., without first running the copy past the airline's corporate communications department. The executive was from another country and did not fully understand the U.S. regulations affecting material announcements. Fortunately, the release was caught in time and submitted to the airline for review prior to its issuance.

In yet another example, which unfortunately was aired over the "wires" a few years ago, one company issued a release claiming that it had been the first to design a particular kind of product in its market. Shortly after the release hit the wires, a competing firm saw the release and issued their own announcement on the same wire service, saying that the first company was wrong, and that as a matter of fact, *they* had introduced the first product in this category. They supplied credible third-party backup in the release to prove their claim.

Clearly the company issuing the first release hadn't taken the time to verify its statements. The end result was that the company looked foolish, although in retrospect, it *should* be pointed out that the wires should never be used to "counter" your competition's claims. A simple editorial alert to the target media would have sufficed without airing the dirty laundry for all to see. This was a great example of where two CEOs' egos got in the way.

At one firm, a well-intentioned executive encouraged staff to "go to the edge" when it came to PR. He felt that the press activities should be daring and bold. This is where his lack of formal PR training, as well as lack of exposure to legal ramifications, clouded his guidance. PR is an area where you should be bold in strategy, but not necessarily in content. There is a difference.

PR professionals face increased scrutiny from government regulatory agencies, consumer groups and the competitors of their clients or companies, according to Michael C. Lasky, a partner at Davis & Gilbert LLP who counsels the nation's leading public relations firms and its executives. "There are significant consequences to the public relations executives and their clients if they issue a statement or claim that is false or misleading," he notes.

"Now more than ever, public relations executives must recognize that their activities are subject to legal regulation and that their marketing activities are commercial speech."

Copying and Website Links

I've noticed on several occasions that younger employees (Generations X and Y) often don't feel the need to obtain permission for website links or copying key press clips in bulk. There are certain regulations affecting both of those activities, so it pays to do the right thing in these instances.

If your company is mentioned in a magazine article, and you wish to post it on your website or link to the magazine itself, obtain permission first. Many magazines require a fee if you want to post the article on your site. If you plan to distribute bulk copies of the article to a sales team, for example, check with the magazine directly. In some cases, you can just put "Copyright (date) Name of Publication" at the bottom of the article before mass-producing it. You thus give fair credit to the magazine. In other instances, the magazine will require a reprint fee. Occasionally, I've had executives question this dedication to details. (See the chapter on Ethics—"Everyone is doing it"). Inevitably, disregard of copyrights will surface, and your image with the magazine will plummet. Can you afford the loss of goodwill? Remember, it's more precious than saving a few pennies on reprint costs.

What Exactly is Sarbanes-Oxley?

The S-O Act was signed into law on July 31, 2002, and is on a multi-year deployment schedule with the vast majority of the "titles" or sections enforced within 12 months of the signing date. Known as the "Corporate Governance Law," it introduced hundreds of new requirements for compliance, reporting, auditing, quality control, and independence, just to name a few areas. The law affects every public company listed on any U.S. Stock Exchange, including foreign companies. For the first time in history, the law holds the individual executives responsible for failures, not just the company itself.

Organizations, along with their CEOs and CFOs, can face up to $15 million in fines and 10-year jail terms for each and every offense that is determined to be gross negligence or intentional fraudulent behavior. Even more ominous, companies and their senior executives can face up to $2 million in fines and two-year sentences for accidental infractions that are deemed avoidable, had proper controls been enforced. The law is very complex, and with all of its amendments and renderings, is more than 500 pages in length, including 11 new compliance titles to SEC codes, more than 90 individual legal sections, and more than 300 discrete and enforceable points of law. Although complex, it does represent an opportunity to apply best practices throughout an entire enterprise, including PR.

"Companies should look at S-O overall, not just in sections," advises Kevin McHolland, a partner with Ernst & Young in Phoenix, Arizona, who has studied the Act extensively. "The Act requires the CEO, executive team and audit committee to have a better understanding of the risks of the company, and really puts more 'teeth' into the law. The identification of key operating information has long been part of a company's approach. What today's economy and Sarbanes-Oxley regulation require is that the executives understand what is happening faster, and in turn inform the board and make not only timely decisions, but full and accurate disclosures."

The types of changes stipulated by S-O can be grouped into three major areas: *certifications,* whereby the CEO and CFO must certify results or face potential criminal and financial penalties; *internal controls management,* in which companies maintain sound internal controls and auditors are required to sign off; and *reporting,* which means accelerated filing deadlines and real-time disclosure of material events. There is a greater emphasis on accuracy of press releases today than ever before.

As an executive and/or PR professional, you need to be doubly sure that your press information is accurate and straight-forward. Careers—and even your freedom—may depend on it.

Chapter 23:

Dealing with Catastrophe: What to Do if Things Go Wrong

———

"If the public and media perceive that your organization is taking the crisis seriously and is dealing with it openly, the storm will pass more quickly. And if the crisis is brought on by company error, a well-placed apology, as bitter as it may taste, will take the air out of the critics."
— Garth Andrews, Manager/Communications,
Southwest Gas Corporation

———

It used to be that the kinds of crises a business might face included power outages, loss of revenue, or product or service safety recalls. Hard to believe that now the list of possible challenges includes acts of terrorism.

Be that as it may, the number one action you can take to handle any catastrophe is to plan for it *before* it happens. Admittedly, planning always sounds like a boring, time-wasting activity. However, crisis plans are *not* difficult to create and have certain recommended components, regardless of the catastrophe.

The following outline suggests guidelines for what your business should include in its crisis plan. You can probably draw one up yourself over a weekend. Keep in mind that the time you spend now will save you money and unnecessary grief when and if the unthinkable happens.

Make a list of your company's key management. One of those management members should be designated as the "crisis team leader." Add to this list key supporting vendors (such as legal counsel, public relations) including their addresses, phone numbers, cell phone numbers and email addresses.

Have a one-page fact sheet on your business and facilities, as reporters often ask for this data when a crisis occurs. Include information on the square footage and age of your building, names of other tenants in the building, information on its owner, the year your company was founded, and the number of employees.

Compile a list of contact information for the local media (TV, newspapers, radio) and local, county, state and federal representatives. Your chamber of commerce may already have such a list prepared. More than likely, they will be willing to share it with you if you indicate your reason for needing it.

Prepare a list of steps that should be followed immediately when a crisis occurs. Some recommendations are:

- The crisis team leader's job is to alert the rest of the crisis team when an incident occurs. That leader will establish a schedule for any regular meetings of the crisis team until the crisis is deemed over, resolved, and/or minimized.

- As a team, meet and determine/agree upon the facts to disseminate to all with a need to know (depending on the type of crisis). These typically would include company employees, community, media (press, radio, TV) and county officials.

- Identify who on the team will be the official "spokes-person" for the company during the crisis. This may or may not be the same person as the crisis team leader.

- Instruct the company receptionist or person handling incoming calls at your business on how and where to direct incoming inquiries during the crisis.

- Set up a special hotline number if the crisis warrants it. If your company has inadvertently polluted the local groundwater, for instance, residents will want to be able to call and receive updated information regarding the problem, how it affects them, what if anything they should do, and steps being taken.

- Keep a log of all incoming inquiries and how they are handled. Write a brief press release, if necessary, to inform the public of the basic details surrounding the incident.

These are the major steps to address a catastrophe. They describe what to do, but not how to do it. *How* you handle the situation will determine the positive or negative image of your company in the long run. There are some tried-and-true media do's and don'ts to remember. Include these tips in the crisis plan, as it is often difficult to remember how to react in the heat of the moment.

- Do not have multiple people speaking on behalf of the company. This can lead to convoluted and contradictory information and messages.

- Return media phone calls as soon as possible. Sometimes if the crisis is severe enough, a company will hold daily press updates.

- If you don't know the answer to a question, say so and tell them you will endeavor to find the answer. Don't speculate.

- Treat the crisis with the somberness it deserves, and avoid minimizing the problem. Some companies hope that by downplaying the incident it will blow over, but this usually just serves to fan the flames of curiosity.

- Treat all conversations with the media and other public officials as "on the record"—never assume, even if you ask them to hold it in confidence, that it will remain so.

- Show compassion and sensitivity. Former New York City Mayor Guiliani and his calm, yet sensitive leadership during September 11 is a wonderful example of how to handle a crisis.

Once the crisis plan is completed, distribute it to your management team and any outside support vendors that might be involved, such as your lawyer, accountant, building owner, service distributor, and so on. An ideal way to communicate the information is to schedule a face-to-face meeting to present the document both in hard copy and electronically. This enables the members to see who else is part of the crisis team, and enables you to explain the purpose of the plan and answer any questions on the spot. Some PR agencies such as Peppercom in New York offer a specialized service that helps clients prepare for and measure their response to a simulated crisis. If you are in an industry that lends itself to multiple types of crisis, using such a service would be a great way to prepare.

The crisis plan is one of the few PR deliverables that you hope you never have to use.

Chapter 24:

Budgeting and Measurement

"We've found that the primary reason that people don't measure is that they are afraid of the results or don't know about the tools. What people don't realize is that they learn far more from measuring failure than they do from showing off their successes."
— Katie Delahaye Paine, CEO,
    KDPaine & Partners

Early in my career, I heard my manager advise the CEO that "PR is never 'free.'" That saying has stayed with me since. It may appear to be free, since it doesn't involve buying space/time in magazines or local radio stations, as you do with advertisements, or creating a trade show booth. But there are various and sundry expenses associated with implementing a successful PR program. Some can be anticipated, some cannot.

Following is a list of typical line items you should include in your budget:

- PC equipment/software—tech support and software upgrades

- Newswire services to distribute your releases
- Media databases and editorial calendar services
- Award submission fees
- Buyer's Guide listing fees
- Photography for case studies and other special occasions (open houses, new product shots)
- Headshots of your executives, company building
- Press kit covers (although these are being used less and less these days)
- Graphic fees to convert files into pdfs or create any artwork on consignment for white papers, etc.
- Monthly clipping fees (print and online)
- Article reprint fees and website permission fees
- Industry analyst subscription fees (these can run in the $60K – $100K annual fee range)
- Freelance writer fees for case studies, white papers (anywhere from $3K – $20K)
- Travel and expenses for press tours, press conferences
- Event fees—open houses
- Webcasts—phone, web meeting platform fees, graphic fees to create invitations and email blasts, speaker fees
- Any sponsorship fees
- Reference directories
- Copies (for clips, press kits, etc.)

PR budgets range from the pitiful to the overkill. Based on my experience and the companies I've worked with over the years, a tentative rule of thumb seems to be $750 – $1,000 for every employee. A 300-employee company, therefore, might have a budget of $225,000 − $300,000, which would include some of the annual industry analyst subscription fees. A 40-employee company would have a more modest budget of $30,000 − $40,000. Some companies also use the formula of 9% − 11% of total revenues for their total marketing budget, of which PR is a subset.

Measurement

There are a few proven ways to measure the effectiveness of your PR efforts. Before any measurement takes place, however, you have to have a baseline from which to start. You need to understand your current company image, both internally and externally, in order to know in which direction to move and how to measure progress.

One recommended way to establish that baseline is to have your PR director or an outside resource conduct phone interviews of key internal employees, key customers, and key media. A summary of these interviews then provides you with a snapshot of where you are.

I've always said that good PR is similar to what a Supreme Court justice once said about pornography—"I can't define it, but I know it when I see it." When a PR program is in full swing, you just know it. You see it in the number of incoming calls you receive from editors, instead of having to race after them to get covered. Your phone calls and emails to the editors are returned promptly. You see it in the quantity and quality of clips coming in monthly. The sales reps are finding that prospects have already heard of your company when they go to call on them. Your corporate website is chock-full of good information for editors and customers alike and is receiving qualified hits. These are the warm fuzzy feelings you get from a strong PR program that has achieved momentum.

But these times call for more than warm fuzzies. As measurement grows, observes PR measurement guru Katie Paine, the times call for data-driven PR, when you make decisions based on quantitative and qualitative results.

She offers the following advice:

Recent technology advances have resulted in vastly improved ways to measure PR. Before any measurement takes place, however, you need to determine two things: where you are now, and where you want to end up.

Determining where you are now requires a baseline. You need to understand your current company image, both internally and externally, and how it compares to the competition-only then can you know in which direction to move and how to measure progress. One recommended way to establish that baseline is to have your PR director or (preferably) an outside resource conduct phone interviews of key internal employees, key customers, and key media. Asking a standard set of questions will give you a snapshot of where you are and provide needed data on which to base your decision. It is also important to know how your audience sees you versus your competitors, so don't forget to include them in the questionnaire.

The second key part of measurement is establishing your objectives. In other words if you want to measure return on investment, you first need to define what the "return" is that you are looking for.

Some typical objectives might be:

- An increase in the number of unique visitors to your website or numbers of leads.

- A greater share of ink or visibility.

- More people having more opportunities to see your key messages.

■ More people more likely to try your product or service.

■ More people aware of your product or service.

Depending on which objectives you chose, you can then select from a variety of measurement techniques that have gained acceptance in recent years.

Share of Voice/Discussion

By tracking the number of times you and your competition are mentioned in a given set of key media, you can determine whether you are receiving your fair share of ink for someone in your industry. By factoring in the circulation figures for the media, you can see whether you're reaching your fair share of audience "eyeballs" as well. This is called "share of voice" or "share of discussion."

Media Content Analysis

If you take the extra step to actually read and analyze the articles that are written about you, you can determine whether they contain your key messages, whether they position you as you want to be seen, and whether they leave a reader more likely to do business with your company. This can provide valuable data that could show which tactics are better at getting your messages across.

Integrated Media Analysis

By tracking your media coverage as well as your web traffic and sales leads, you can determine what PR activities are contributing to any increases or decreases you might see.

Online Surveys

Technology has also brought the cost of surveys down, with companies like SurveyMonkey and Zoomerang providing free or nearly free services. Anyone with access to a list of email addresses of customers can pull together a survey in about an hour. Such surveys can help you determine your level of awareness and preference, as well as how your constituencies perceive you.

Online Image Analysis

With the explosion in consumer generated media, you can frequently listen in on what your customers are saying about you just by reading the postings about you. This is a great measure of whether you're getting your messages out and whether you are changing any perceptions. Just go to Technorati or Sphere and search on your brand, as well as your competitor's brand, to get data on how the online community is responding to your efforts.

Frequently Asked Questions about Measurement

Q: How do you "account for" avoiding negative press—in other words, how do I get credit for keeping our name out of a bad article?

A: Assuming you have some sort of media measurement program in place, you should be looking at your share of negative press—in other words, of all the negative press that gets written about your industry, what share is yours? By benchmarking yourself against peer companies you'll be able to determine how effective you are at keeping the bad press at bay.

Q: Why should I put measurement into the budget?

A: Who needs a budget? There are lots of ways to measure without any budget at all. Both Cyberalert and Customscoop offer free two-week trials. Google News is free. Both can give your PR manager the data he/she needs to make better decisions. Also, don't forget about the data that you already have somewhere in the organization—whether it's from sales, customer satisfaction, your webmaster or finance. Incorporate that into your report to demonstrate outcomes such as web traffic or sales leads. Once you've demonstrated the power and the usefulness of measurement, it will end up in next year's budget.

Q: How do you calculate impressions for online media and blogs?

A: Most of the time you can't. At the moment, there are no audited consistent "impression" numbers for most blogs or for many online media sites. Comscore offers a fair number of website circulation figures but they are by no means all-inclusive.

Q: How do you define "positive and negative" coverage?

A: When KDPaine & Partners analyzes media coverage, we use a criteria agreed upon with clients that is generally something such as: Does the article leave the reader more or less likely to do business with the company? If it's a non-profit NGO or lobbying organization, it might be, "Does the article leave the reader more likely to support the cause?" In the case of a government public affairs organization it might be, "Does the article leave the reader more or less likely to comply with the law or policy?"

Q: Why isn't there a standard for PR measurement?

A: Because PR means public relations and deals with relationships with publics. Every organization has different goals and different publics, so it's very hard to come up with a single metric that applies to all organizations. In Canada, there's the "MRP" standard that was developed by a CPRS and a group of practitioners but it only deals with media metrics, not relationship measures.

If your PR program isn't gaining traction, any number of things could be wrong. Here's where subsequent interviews, both internally and externally, 12 months later might be helpful as a comparison. Reasons might include:

- Your product is the problem (this is often the case, rather than the PR efforts, but it may be difficult for executives to admit to or even realize).

- You're targeting the wrong markets—maybe you chose a vertical market that is traditionally slow to adopt new technology.

- The information you're delivering to the media is not considered interesting/newsy, helpful or enlightening.

- As the executive, you're directing the PR efforts too closely; maybe you should back away and let the PR director take the helm—after all, that's why you hired him/her, right?

The instinctive reaction is to fire the PR director or agency, but often the problem is not the director, but an error in the company strategy or business proposition. PR is not the ubiquitous "Elmer's Glue" of marketing...it can't help if the materials you're working with are as inappropriate as trying to glue metal.

Chapter 25:

A Few Words About Ethics

"Whether you manage the public relations profession full-time, or dabble in the field occasionally, you will find that practicing sound public relations ethics will make your customers, business partners and employees more trusting and loyal to your organization, resulting in a more successful operation."
— Linda Welter Cohen, APR, 2006 Chair,
  Public Relations Society of America Board of Ethics
  & Professional Standards

Unfortunately, public relations practitioners will encounter many questionable activities during their careers. In anticipation of these challenges, the professional association for the industry (Public Relations Society of America) has developed and published a code of ethics, which sets the standards and guidelines that direct the practice of PR. (See appendix of this book for the full text of the PRSA Code of Ethics).

The primary catalyst for these uncomfortable situations is the discrepancy in perception between executive management and PR counsel about the definition of PR and how it should be carried out. This discrepancy causes uninformed executives to cross the line from positive positioning to deception, in which the attempt is made to manipulate public opinion through false information or alternatively, through non-disclosure.

As we've noted, PR counsel realistically should be on strategic equal footing with the rest of management. Many, if not most executives, however, mistakenly view the PR person's role as part of the employee contract that the employee undertakes when signing on with the corporation. Subsequently, executives may argue that the PR agent has a fiduciary relationship with the corporation, which means he/she must be loyal and obedient and must act in the best interests of the corporation. Or if it is a written contract between a PR agency and the corporation, the executive may contend that the agency is not fulfilling its performance as outlined in the contract, if it chooses not to follow his or her instructions.

It is important for those directing the PR activities, however, to realize that the PR professional's duty, both legally and ethically, is only to obey *reasonable* requests or guidance. The agent is not required to follow through on anything illegal.[1] One might argue that it is unclear who in a corporation is charged with the authority to define what is legal or ethical. In the case of corporate communications to a wide range of audiences, such as investment bankers, shareholders, or the media, it is clearly the PR executive who has a so-called duty of care in his/her role as PR expert or counsel. No one else will be as ardently looking out for the reputation and credibility, not only of the PR individual but of the corporation as a whole.

Admittedly, the degree to which PR practitioners feel comfortable in a "watchdog" role varies. Agencies, for example, may enjoy comparatively more leeway than in-house PR professionals because they are not directly employed by the corporation. Yet, they may still act unethically for fear of losing the business. Alternatively, in-house PR counsel may be reluctant to voice strong opinions for fear of the repercussions, which might be as severe as losing a job.

Warning Signs for Unethical Behavior

PR directors can safely assume that they will face multiple instances of unethical business behavior during their careers. On a positive note, much of this behavior can be predicted and anticipated, as there are generally accepted warning signs that unethical behavior is about to be committed, or is at least being contemplated. Compiled from the textbook on business law and ethics by Marianne Jennings, a noted expert and columnist on business ethics, as well as from the ethics website for the Josephson Institute, the following list represents a fairly comprehensive compilation of likely statements that should serve as warning signs:

- If it's necessary, it's ethical.
- If it's legal and permissible, it's okay.
- I was doing it for you.
- I was just following orders.
- It's all for a good cause.
- The system is unfair.
- I'm just fighting fire with fire.
- It doesn't hurt anyone.
- If I don't do it, someone else will.
- Everyone is doing it.
- It's OK as long as the end goal is ethical.[2]

All of these defenses serve as strong indications that executives are focusing on short-term goals, such as increased revenue, rather than on the long-term implications of their actions.

The PRSA code of ethics was updated in 2000 and includes specific examples of improper conduct. As an executive or PR professional, it behooves you to review these examples and keep them in mind when faced with questionable situations.

Among the most common errors I have seen are:

- Offering an editor or analyst "free" product, even if the intentions are good.

- "Lying by omission"—failing to advise an editor or analyst of connections or facts that might not present the company in the best light.

- Calling the competition under the guise of a "student" who is seeking more information about the company.

- Writing a release or case study in such a way that the full truth is not evident or is glossed over.

Executives should hold themselves and their PR representatives to a higher standard, and ensure that their communication to the outside world is "utterly transparent."

Sample Ethical Frameworks

There are three premises in particular that are useful in establishing an ethical framework for your company. The **Golden Rule** approach, for example, espouses behavior based on the "do unto others as you would have them do unto you" philosophy. Under this guideline, PR professionals would consider how they would feel if the situation were reversed, and they were on the receiving end of the action. This often puts a questionable situation into clearer perspective.

The **newspaper headline** theory asks professionals to imagine how comfortable they might feel with a published newspaper account of the action they are about to take. Under this model, PR counsel would imagine the impact that a public description of their action (or the corporation's action) might have. Many situations that seem innocent can take on dangerous implications when rendered in print. In the public court of opinion, as it is said, perception is often reality. Can the corporation risk a damaging perception?

There is also a **proposed ethical framework** devised by law professor Gwendolyne Parks, which lays out various aspects to evaluate. First, a professional should decide if there is a disagreement over facts or over conceptual issues. The latter, such as "hot topic areas" including abortion, stem cell research, and gun rights, are very difficult to change. A professional should then analyze the situation according to his or her own professional standards, respect for persons, and commonly accepted moral standards, as well as other aspects of unique importance to them.[3]

It is an inescapable fact that the public relations profession, because it is acting on behalf of another, is more likely to encounter legal and ethical controversies where an individual's personal value system clashes with that of the organization they are representing. Rather than wait for the inevitable to happen, however, PR practitioners are well-advised to be introspective up front and to draw up a blueprint of how they will act when faced with such dilemmas.

Chapter 26:

Conclusion

"Life's but a walking shadow, a poor player,
That struts and frets his hour upon the stage,
And then is heard no more; it is a tale
Told by an idiot, full of sound and fury,
Signifying nothing."
(Macbeth, V, v, 24).

There are many books available that explain in great detail the steps behind crafting various public relations deliverables. Although this guide touches on some of the how-to's, it is primarily intended to explain the "why" behind the steps. It is hoped that after reading this guide, an executive, public relations professional, or student begins to realize that PR is a powerful yet often misunderstood (and misapplied!) marketing approach.

PR is an integral part not only of the other marketing communications practices, but of the corporation as a whole. To be most effective, it must work closely with other functions such as research and development, human resources, and finance.

If you can construct your PR program ethically and accurately, and if you can remember that you serve yourself best by serving the analyst's or editor's needs first, you will surpass the majority of companies in the market who are trying to make themselves heard.

By realizing there is more to a PR strategy than merely issuing press releases, you will avoid being guilty of the fate described in *Macbeth* when you deliver press releases "told by an idiot, full of sound and fury, signifying nothing."

###

Appendix A:

Public Relations Society of America

Code of Ethics Preamble

Public Relations Society of America Member Code of Ethics 2000

- Professional Values
- Principles of Conduct
- Commitment and Compliance

This Code applies to PRSA members. The Code is designed to be a useful guide for PRSA members as they carry out their ethical responsibilities. This document is designed to anticipate and accommodate, by precedent, ethical challenges that may arise. The scenarios outlined in the Code provision are actual examples of misconduct. More will be added as experience with the Code occurs.

The Public Relations Society of America (PRSA) is committed to ethical practices. The level of public trust PRSA members seek, as we serve the public good, means we have taken on a special obligation to operate ethically.

The value of member reputation depends upon the ethical conduct of everyone affiliated with the Public Relations Society of America. Each of us sets an example for each other—as well as other professionals—by our pursuit of excellence with powerful standards of performance, professionalism, and ethical conduct.

Emphasis on enforcement of the Code has been eliminated. But, the PRSA Board of Directors retains the right to bar from membership or expel from the Society any individual who has been or is sanctioned by a government agency or convicted in a court of law of an action that is in violation of this Code.

Ethical practice is the most important obligation of a PRSA member. We view the Member Code of Ethics as a model for other professions, organizations, and professionals.

This statement presents the core values of PRSA members and, more broadly, of the public relations profession. These values provide the foundation for the Member Code of Ethics and set the industry standard for the professional practice of public relations. These values are the fundamental beliefs that guide our behaviors and decision-making process. We believe our professional values are vital to the integrity of the profession as a whole.

ADVOCACY

We serve the public interest by acting as responsible advocates for those we represent. We provide a voice in the marketplace of ideas, facts, and viewpoints to aid informed public debate.

HONESTY

We adhere to the highest standards of accuracy and truth in advancing the interests of those we represent and in communicating with the public.

EXPERTISE

We acquire and responsibly use specialized knowledge and experience. We advance the profession through continued professional development, research, and education. We build mutual understanding, credibility, and relationships among a wide array of institutions and audiences.

INDEPENDENCE

We provide objective counsel to those we represent. We are accountable for our actions.

LOYALTY

We are faithful to those we represent, while honoring our obligation to serve the public interest.

FAIRNESS

We deal fairly with clients, employers, competitors, peers, vendors, the media, and the general public. We respect all opinions and support the right of free expression.

FLOW OF INFORMATION

Core Principle

Protecting and advancing the free flow of accurate and truthful information is essential to serving the public interest and contributing to informed decision making in a democratic society.

Intent

- To maintain the integrity of relationships with the media, government officials, and the public.

- To aid informed decision-making.

Guidelines

A member shall:

- Preserve the integrity of the process of communication.

- Be honest and accurate in all communications.

- Act promptly to correct erroneous communications for which the practitioner is responsible.

- Preserve the free flow of unprejudiced information when giving or receiving gifts by ensuring that gifts are nominal, legal, and infrequent.

Examples of Improper Conduct Under this Provision:

- A member representing a ski manufacturer gives a pair of expensive racing skis to a sports magazine columnist, to influence the columnist to write favorable articles about the product.

- A member entertains a government official beyond legal limits and/or in violation of government reporting requirements.

COMPETITION

Core Principle

Promoting healthy and fair competition among professionals preserves an ethical climate while fostering a robust business environment.

Intent

- To promote respect and fair competition among public relations professionals.

- To serve the public interest by providing the widest choice of practitioner options.

Guidelines

A member shall:
- Follow ethical hiring practices designed to respect free and open competition without deliberately undermining a competitor.

- Preserve intellectual property rights in the marketplace.

Examples of Improper Conduct Under This Provision:

- A member employed by a "client organization" shares helpful information with a counseling firm that is competing with others for the organization's business.

- A member spreads malicious and unfounded rumors about a competitor in order to alienate the competitor's clients and employees in a ploy to recruit people and business.

DISCLOSURE OF INFORMATION

Core Principle

Open communication fosters informed decision making in a democratic society.

Intent

- To build trust with the public by revealing all information needed for responsible decision making.

Guidelines

A member shall:

- Be honest and accurate in all communications.

- Act promptly to correct erroneous communications for which the member is responsible.

- Investigate the truthfulness and accuracy of information released on behalf of those represented.

- Reveal the sponsors for causes and interests represented.

- Disclose financial interest (such as stock ownership) in a client's organization.

- Avoid deceptive practices.

Examples of Improper Conduct Under this Provision:

- Front groups: A member implements "grass roots" campaigns or letter-writing campaigns to legislators on behalf of undisclosed interest groups.

- Lying by omission: A practitioner for a corporation knowingly fails to release financial information, giving a misleading impression of the corporation's performance.

- A member discovers inaccurate information disseminated via a Web site or media kit and does not correct the information.

- A member deceives the public by employing people to pose as volunteers to speak at public hearings and participate in "grass roots" campaigns.

SAFEGUARDING CONFIDENCES

Core Principle

Client trust requires appropriate protection of confidential and private information.

Intent

- To protect the privacy rights of clients, organizations, and individuals by safeguarding confidential information.

Guidelines

A member shall:

- Safeguard the confidences and privacy rights of present, former, and prospective clients and employees.

- Protect privileged, confidential, or insider information gained from a client or organization.

- Immediately advise an appropriate authority if a member discovers that confidential information is being divulged by an employee of a client company or organization.

Examples of Improper Conduct Under This Provision:

- A member changes jobs, takes confidential information, and uses that information in the new position to the detriment of the former employer.

- A member intentionally leaks proprietary information to the detriment of some other party.

CONFLICTS OF INTEREST

Core Principle

Avoiding real, potential or perceived conflicts of interest builds the trust of clients, employers, and the publics.

Intent

- To earn trust and mutual respect with clients or employers.

- To build trust with the public by avoiding or ending situations that put one's personal or professional interests in conflict with society's interests.

Guidelines

A member shall:
- Act in the best interests of the client or employer, even subordinating the member's personal interests.

- Avoid actions and circumstances that may appear to compromise good business judgment or create a conflict between personal and professional interests.

- Disclose promptly any existing or potential conflict of interest to affected clients or organizations.

- Encourage clients and customers to determine if a conflict exists after notifying all affected parties.

Examples of Improper Conduct Under This Provision

- The member fails to disclose that he or she has a strong financial interest in a client's chief competitor.

- The member represents a "competitor company" or a "conflicting interest" without informing a prospective client.

ENHANCING THE PROFESSION

Core Principle

Public relations professionals work constantly to strengthen the public's trust in the profession.

Intent

- To build respect and credibility with the public for the profession of public relations.

- To improve, adapt and expand professional practices.

Guidelines

A member shall:

- Acknowledge that there is an obligation to protect and enhance the profession.

- Keep informed and educated about practices in the profession to ensure ethical conduct.

- Actively pursue personal professional development.

- Decline representation of clients or organizations that urge or require actions contrary to this Code.

- Accurately define what public relations activities can accomplish.

- Counsel subordinates in proper ethical decision making.

- Require that subordinates adhere to the ethical requirements of the Code.

- Report ethical violations, whether committed by PRSA members or not, to the appropriate authority.

Examples of Improper Conduct Under This Provision:

- A PRSA member declares publicly that a product the client sells is safe, without disclosing evidence to the contrary.

- A member initially assigns some questionable client work to a non-member practitioner to avoid the ethical obligation of PRSA membership.

Appendix B:

Resource Directory of Web Links

Following is a partial list of PR-related resources:

General wire services—for distributing your releases

- Businesswire: www.businesswire.com
- Marketwire: www.marketwire.com
- PrimeNewswire: www.primenewsire.com
- PR Newswire: www.prnewswire.com

Clipping services—for obtaining all print/web mentions of your company

- Bacon's: www.bacons.com
- Burrelle's/Luce: www.burrellesluce.com
- Ewatch: www.prnewswire.com
- Lexis Nexis: www.lexisnexis.com

Media/Analyst directories—lists of media and/or editorial calendars for various vertical markets

- Bacon's Media Source: www.bacons.com
- CornerBar PR: www.cornerbarpr.com
- FinderBinder: www.finderbinder.com
- MediaFinder: www.mediafinder.com
- PRSourceCode (IT markets only): www.prsourcecode.com
- SRDS: www.srds.com
- Tekrati: www.tekrati.com
- Vocus: www.vocus.com

Style books—reference for press release style

- AP (Associated Press) Style book: www.apstylebook.com
- Chicago Manual of Style: www.chicagomanualofstyle.org

RSS services

- BlogLines: www.bloglines.com
- FeedDemon: www.feeddemon.com
- My Yahoo: www.my.yahoo.com
- NewsGator: www.newsgator.com
- Net Newswire: www.netnewswire.com

Blog search engines

- Blog Pulse: www.blogpulse.com
- Sphere: www.sphere.com
- Technorati: www.technorati.com

Wikis

- New PR Wiki: www.newprwiki.com/wiki/pmwiki.php
- Wikipedia: www.wikipedia.org

Survey tools

- Survey Monkey: www.surveymonkey.com
- Zoomerang: www.zoomerang.com

PR measurement—resources for measuring the media and word-of-mouth success of your PR program

- Biz360: www.biz360.com
- Comscore: www.comscore.com
- Custom Scoop: www.customscoop.com
- Cyberalert: www.cyberalert.com
- Delahaye/MediaLink: www.medialink.com
- KDPaine & Partners: www.measuresofsuccess.com
- Neilsen Buzzmetrics: www.nielsenbuzzmetrics.com

Professional associations—industry associations that are relevant to PR

- International Association of Business Communicators: www.iabc.com
- Public Relations Society of America: www.prsa.org

Websites with good tips—helpful tips on how to work with the press

- "Care and Feeding of the Press": www.netpress.org

Customer (editor) relationship packages—software packages to maintain your list of editors and analysts

- Act!: www.act.com
- Bacon's MediaMap: www.bacons.com
- Vocus Software: www.vocus.com

Media trainers—professionals who provide executive media training

- Roy Heffley, Moomey Communications: www.moomey.com

Speaking organizations

- Dale Carnegie: www.dalecarnegietraining.com
- Toastmasters: www.toastmasters.org

Sample magazines and newsletters

- Communication Briefings: www.combriefings.com
- Interactive Public Relations: www.odwyerpr.com
- Jack O'Dwyer's Newsletter: www.odwyerpr.com
- O'Dwyer's PR Daily (online): www.odwyerpr.com
- PR News: www.prandmarketing.com
- PR Reporter: www.ragan.com
- PR Week: www.prweek.com
- Public Relations Tactics: www.prsa.org
- Ragan's Media Relations Report: www.ragan.com
- The Holmes Report www.holmesreport.com
- The Public Relations Strategist: www.prsa.org
- The Ragan Report: www.ragan.com

Appendix C:
Sample PR Deliverables

The following are samples of some of the PR deliverables mentioned in this guide:

> *A. Company Backgrounder – following is a sample of a company backgrounder for a software company. Note that the writing style is factual and straightforward, not salesy or promotional. It is often helpful to include objective, third-party industry or analyst data to help describe market size, trends and drivers. Backgrounders can be written for industry editors already somewhat familiar with a market and its acronyms, such as this one, or on a more general level for a wider, non-technical audience.*

TELEDIRECT INTERNATIONAL, INC.

Corporate Backgrounder

Overview
Founded in 1983 and headquartered in Scottsdale, Arizona, TeleDirect International, Inc. is a privately held company that provides customer campaign management and automated marketing software designed to increase revenues for enterprises' sales and customer service centers. Companies and teleservices outsourcing firms employing TeleDirect products and services enjoy the advantages of a scalable, open solution that combines advanced computer telephony technology with powerful desktop software for customer campaign automation and dialogue management.

TeleDirect's customer base includes leading companies in the communications services, travel and leisure, newspaper publishing, healthcare and financial services markets. These industries in particular utilize a large number of in-house call center agents, or contract with external teleservices firms, in order to provide one-to-one service and support and to sell goods and services to businesses and consumers. The company's flagship product, Liberation® 6000, enables an enterprise to quickly mobilize and equip its agents for maximum productivity, effectiveness, and return on investment. The latest upgrade to Liberation 6000 delivers critical FTC/FCC compliance enhancements to ensure absolute compliance and to simplify accurate tracking and reporting.

Major benefits to customers include:

- **Improved revenue** through highly targeted and effective sales campaigns, improved up-sell/cross-sell success, and improved service levels.

- **Contained costs** through mitigated liabilities and risks of compliance with federal, state and local telemarketing laws; reduced staffing by optimizing the availability and performance of agents; reduced day-to-day involvement of IT and the capital investment and operating costs required to implement campaigns; and extension of existing legacy systems through open standards and flexible integration.

- **Improved customer service**, as the result of the agent's increased focus; reduced number of calls required to complete telephone transactions; and embedded intelligence in the dialog guide to remove agent error and discretion.

- **Improved compliance** with the do-not-call registry and predictive dialer laws, through TeleDirect's ConsumerCare™ approach, which provides performance without annoyance.

Market Overview

The primary driver for enterprises and outsourcing firms that generate sales and deliver support via customer contact centers is revenue generation. Over the last year, enterprises have resumed their focus on identifying and implementing services that will immediately increase revenues through quality customer identification and retention. This focus is in contrast to the market emphasis of the late 90s, when significant investments were made in Internet infrastructure, ecommerce, and CRM (customer relationship management) software. Facing an unpredictable economy, however, enterprises are now turning to technology that can help them increase revenues.

Datamonitor predicts that the global market for call center component technologies—ACDs, CTI, IVR, predictive dialing and call recording—is primed for growth. North America will see a revenue growth rate of 3.8%; the North American market for call center component technologies will reach $3.2 billion by 2007, up from $2.7 billion in 2002. The European call center component market will see annual growth rate of 8.5%; the market is expected to reach revenues of $1.5 billion by 2007.

In 2002, the American Teleservices Association conducted a survey of 1,000 consumers on their use of the telephone. While the Internet seems to be matching the telephone for consumer purchases, teleservices companies continue to play a major role in the sales process. An increasing number of teleservices companies are offering multi-channel customer support—traditional phone-based call centers are diversifying and applying their customer service skills in new ways. Many teleservices companies now offer email, web chat, and ecommerce customer support services. This business model allows Internet sellers to focus on selling, supported by the well-tested sales and service skills of call centers nationwide. (www.ataconnect.org)

The TeleDirect Difference:
The markets of predictive dialing/customer campaign management solutions are crowded with companies who are focusing on a technology sale, but with no real understanding of the unique requirements of call center campaigns. The TeleDirect differentiators can be summed up as the following:

- *Call center-centric solutions*—TeleDirect's solutions were designed from the beginning to produce a higher rate of contact and more sales per agent with less consumer annoyance.

- *Expertise* in the needs of those entrepreneurial enterprises who leverage customer contact centers to increase customer value—TeleDirect knows the nuances of these enterprises, whether they're in communication services, travel and leisure, or publishing. The company's technology has integral features and functions designed specifically for these industries.

■ *Software that does not require IT intervention to change*, but instead can be easily adapted by the marketing or sales manager—Users can create and dynamically adapt their own marketing campaigns to respond to market changes, saving time and money.

Technology Philosophy

TeleDirect's technology approach mirrors its corporate customer-driven philosophy of listening to customers and responding with the appropriate products and improvements, based on their continuous feedback.

Open Systems Technology

TeleDirect embraces an open systems architecture to ensure that the information can be shared easily with other systems across different platforms. This open approach ensures universal connectivity to virtually any database, network and host environment. The object-oriented logic for the non-programmer enables the teleservices manager at a call center to use a powerful Dialog Wizard (graphical programmer interface) to create customized Dialog Guides (scripts). The technology also facilitates comprehensive management and reporting functionality for the teleservices manager to manage and measure all aspects of a particular sales campaign, including agent and group performance statistics.

Patents

TeleDirect has patents on the following technologies:

■ Dialog Wizard – Call Center Agent Interface and Development Tool (patent #6,100,891)

■ Instant Cut-through of Call and Record – Method and Apparatus for Automatic Telephone Scheduling System (patent #5,297,195)

Products and Services for Customer Campaign Management

Liberation 6000 software includes everything a call center needs to develop, implement and manage successful sales campaigns to increase revenues and maintain compliance with changing federal and state regulations. With this solution, marketing and teleservices managers can leverage customer and prospect information stored in their data warehouses to create, launch and monitor marketing campaigns in their multi-channel customer contact centers.

Unlike simple scripting tools and expensive custom software that lack the required functionality and flexibility, Liberation 6000 includes a powerful Dialog Wizard. This feature makes it easy to build and maintain highly customizable screens that enable agents to easily navigate through the sales campaign, clearly articulate important information to the called party, and leverage each and every sales and service contact.

Liberation 6000 is easily scalable for call centers that range from a handful of seats to over 500 seats. The software includes the following components:

Front end:

- *CampaignManager*, serving as the manager's desktop

- *DialogGuide*, acting as the graphical user interface for the agent's desktop

- *DialogWizard*, enabling application development of the scripting

Back end:

- *Computer telephony server*, based on the S.100, H.100 and SCA standards to protect investments made in telephony technology

- *Microsoft SQL database*

- *Direct access*, providing the communication between the (Dialog Guide) and the customer's enterprise information system, such as Customer Relationship Management (CRM) System, Billing/Ordering System, Operations Support System (OSS), Web Servers, and/or Mail Servers.

Optional services to expand the services are also available, such as third-party connect, instant verification, play recorded message, and dynamic campaign blending.

In fall 2003, TeleDirect launched Liberation 6000 v. 6.2.6, a major upgrade that includes enhancements to the graphical user interface throughout, as well as features designed to make it easier than ever to maintain compliance with all state and federal regulations; monitor statistics in real-time from a web browser; and switch from campaign manager to campaign commander mode to administer multiple platforms.

Domain Expertise
TeleDirect's employees have an extensive background in both the front end (agent) and back end (computer telephony) requirements of call center environments. This expertise has helped create products that can be easily adapted to a call center's unique campaign needs, and which do not require expensive, custom programming. This expertise has also ensured that TeleDirect customers have more freedom in their call center operations, as unlike many predictive dialer solutions on the market, for example, Liberation 6000 does not force call centers to disable answering machine detection in order to adhere to new FTC/FCC compliance requirements.

Alliances
TeleDirect has alliances and partnerships with the following companies:

- Microsoft—technology partner (open systems, and database and networking architecture)

- Siemens—strategic channel partner

- Intel—technology partner for middleware and computer telephony

- Inter-Tel—channel provider/distributor

Company History and Philosophy
While many predictive dialing competitors have come and gone over the years, TeleDirect has been in the business of helping end users increase revenues through automated call center technology since 1983.

The company originally was founded in Iowa as a provider of automated call centers. CEO Kathleen Kelly came on board in 1987 and helped commercialize the company's product on a nationwide basis. She was also instrumental in overseeing several critically important business decisions that have propelled the company to its leadership position providing customer campaign management services to the communication services, travel and leisure, and publishing industries.

The company's pivotal shift came in 1997 when TeleDirect, realizing the market drivers towards open standards and greater flexibility for marketing managers, rewrote its technology on an open systems platform. The company expanded beyond a dialer company to include sophisticated but easy-to-use customer campaign management software. Consequently, TeleDirect was able to establish a market niche that separated it from strictly dialer vendors who provided hard-to-customize, proprietary software, as well as from enterprise automation marketing vendors who focused on campaign management for direct mail and related marketing campaigns, instead of call center-centric campaigns.

In 1999, the company relocated its headquarters from Iowa to Scottsdale, Arizona in order to take advantage of the IT and engineering talent pool and Arizona's emerging call center market.

Future Directions

TeleDirect will continue to develop technology and services that focus on helping customers increase revenues through integrated, advanced dialing technology and customer campaign management software.

Management

Kathleen Kelly – President and CEO
Rita Dearing – Chief Operating Officer
Jay Mayne – Chief Financial Officer
Mark Moore – Chief Technology Officer
Tom Buiel – Vice President of Sales

Board of Directors and Advisors

In addition, TeleDirect draws on a strong board of directors with executive management experience in business operations, as well as advanced degrees in management and corporate finance.

Information

For more information, contact TeleDirect at 480-585 6464, or visit the website at www.tdirect.com. The company is located at 17255 N. 82nd Street, Scottsdale, Arizona, 85255.

###

Liberation 6000, DialogWizard, DialogGuide, and CampaignManager are trademarks of TeleDirect International, Inc.

B. *Press Release – following is an example of a press release to announce an event. The combination of a film festival and the national theme of Home Movie Day creates newsworthiness for a local audience.*

Contact:

Mark Rukavina   Linda VandeVrede

iMemories   VandeVrede Public Relations, LLC

cell: 602–680–8011   cell: 480–603–5369

FOR IMMEDIATE RELEASE

**SCOTTSDALE'S iMEMORIES TO HOST METRO PHOENIX'
FIRST ANNUAL "HOME MOVIE DAY"
AT ITS DIGITAL STUDIO:
PUBLIC INVITED TO FREE EVENT**

*All-day Event Saturday, August 12th is Part of Worldwide Celebration
of Amateur Films and Filmmaking*

Scottsdale, Ariz., August 7, 2006 – iMemories today announced that it will be commemorating the worldwide "Home Movie Day" celebration by hosting the event locally at its Scottsdale-based studio. The planned festivities mark the first time ever that metro Phoenix will host this event, which was started in 2003 by a group of film archivists who were concerned about the preservation of home movies shot on film during the 20th century.

Following are the details:

Where: iMemories, 9181 East Bell Road, Suite 101 (Loop 101
                & Bell Road, located next to Alltel Ice Den, North
                Scottsdale)

When: Saturday, August 12, 2006 10:00 a.m. – 6:00 p.m.

What: Visitors to the studio will be able to engage in a variety
                of activities designed to enlighten and entertain, including:

       ■ Watching their own home movies on professional
         16mm, 8mm and Super 8 projectors in a special
         "home theater" screening area

- Getting their home movie film cleaned and inspected
- Talking to iMemories' on-site experts in film archiving, preservation & editing
- Learning the benefits of digitally mastering home movie film
- Refreshments will be served

"Home Movie Day is the once a year 'premiere' for the home movie film reels each one of us has in that dusty box sitting in the closet, garage or off-site storage," said Mark Rukavina, founder & CEO of iMemories. "In that box is every family's most priceless moments, waiting to evoke laughter and tears. iMemories wants to be a part of this celebration of life, as it was recorded and lived. These are the true American 'indie' films."

About the Annual Home Movie Day

Home Movie Day is a worldwide celebration in more than 60 cities of amateur films and filmmaking, and is held annually on the second Saturday in August. These events provide an opportunity for individuals and families to learn more about their own family movies, how to care for films, and how home movies have helped capture 20th century history. For more information, visit www.homemovieday.com or contact Katie Trainor, co-founder of Home Movie Day, at 646-753-1385.

About iMemories

iMemories gives consumers an easy way to preserve and enjoy the priceless moments they've captured over the years in home movies, videotapes and photographs. The Scottsdale, Ariz.-based company uses state-of-the-art technology and techniques to digitally master old film footage and photos to crystal-clear digital media and create dynamic, cinema-quality productions for special occasions. iMemories is located in North Scottsdale at 9181 E. Bell Road in Scottsdale, Ariz., Loop 101 & Bell Road next to the Alltel Ice Den. For more information, visit www.imemories.com or call 480-767-2510 or email service@imemories.com.

C. *White Paper – following is an example of a white paper used to explain a concept in the electric utility industry. White papers are used as informative, academic papers that typically explain a concept or trend in the industry. They can be formatted as straight text, or with minimal graphics in order to keep the informational and academic mission intact. Too many graphics and photos turn it into more of a sales brochure, and therefore less credible.*

It's Time for "Real Time"

When is the right time for "real time" information? Few industries are as dynamic as the electric utility world. Whether markets worldwide are practicing regulated operations, deregulated operations, or are in the process of deregulating, real time data has never been more critical to the success of an organization than it is today.

These organizations are forced to respond to real time changes in their business such as dynamically changing energy prices, loss of generation, failure of transmission and distribution infrastructure, and unplanned electricity demand. How they sense, analyze, and respond to these situations is the difference between your lights working or not. Central to each phase of this problem resolution is real time data. Real time data allows asset owners to identify the problem when it happens, and often, real time data analysis can also help organizations become more proactive, avoiding costly failures altogether.

Just as challenging as the market is the efficiency with which these often geographically distributed organizations operate and communicate. While some companies own assets that operate in all phases of the power industry, such as generation, transmission, distribution, and fuel, these can actually be operated as separate companies within the company. Other asset owners such as independent power producers may own and operate only power generation assets. No matter the organization, it is imperative that all phases of the power industry are in sync, in real time.

These organizations are faced with shrinking budgets and work forces while the demand for their products and services conversely increase. It's been noted that on average, IT spend for utilities is approximately 3% of annual revenues. However, you can most certainly assume that technology plays some key role in almost all of their revenue-associated operations. This just proves that the type of technology you invest in and how you leverage it are multiplying factors in the return on that investment.

Since power is a dynamic product that is difficult to store, it must be produced to meet the real-time demand for that power. This represents the volatility of power generation, transmission, and distribution. If too much or too little power is produced, this can upset the transmission and distribution grids and often results in power outages for consumers. In addition, generators and grid operators often suffer significant financial penalties for non-compliance to scheduled production.

For example, a local Independent System Operator (ISO) forecasts the amount of electricity required by consumers for the next day, and even within the day, the ISO dynamically modifies forecasts and communicates new power requirements generally in 10- or 15-minute increments. The generator is to follow this forecast as closely as possible. If the generator makes too much power, that power is usually not purchased and is essentially "free," but if the generator produces too little power, they must purchase additional power in spot markets to cover their deficiency. This usually costs the generator a premium, on top of already lost revenues for that same power. The RTOs and ISOs—those responsible for predicting how much power will be used in a given way—need to be extremely good at their predictions. Planning, forecasting, and operations are key functions and all of the elements have to work together.

But, even the best forecasts cannot account for unplanned outages or shortages of power. Real time information, however, can change that seemingly negative situation into a revenue opportunity. As an example, a generation dispatcher who is monitoring key performance indicators for his assets is also monitoring key metrics of the transmission grid. He notices the telltale sign of a frequency disturbance, which indicates a power generation station has shut down abruptly. The generation dispatcher immediately contacts his peer at the energy trading desk and informs him of the event. The trader can check the real time operations of his assets against the committed schedule for those same assets. In real time, he is able to determine that he has additional power that he can sell into the market to cover the loss of generation. While the trader makes that deal, the generation dispatcher communicates the need to increase power generation, all in real time. The generation company not only realizes more revenue through additional power sales, but this latest sale also pays a premium for mitigating the loss of other generation.

Real time data also plays a key part of a practice called "economic dispatch." In our example above, we demonstrated how providing the right information to the right person, in real time, allowed them to take advantage of an otherwise undetected revenue opportunity. What if you could actually maximize that revenue opportunity even more by knowing which asset to dispatch to produce the power with the lowest operating costs? That's economic dispatch. By understanding financial performance indicators from within our business and from outside, we can make more profitable decisions. If you understand how much you are currently paying for fuels, how much practices such as maintenance affect your operating costs, and the overall asset efficiency, you can determine which asset can produce the next increment of power at the widest profit margin.

Asset management, or more specifically maintenance, often consumes 30% or more of a company's operating budget. Monitoring asset performance in real time improves reliability, availability, and capacity of assets, which means you operate more frequently and in prime revenue windows. For example, a 1% reduction of asset forced outages is not only realistic, but would result in savings of several millions of dollars in lost revenues alone for most mid-sized power companies. A simple example of monitoring key operations efficiency metrics could provide the right people with information that a critical asset is about to fail. It's much easier to mitigate a problem before it happens than after it results in a failure.

Business "intelligence" is the culmination of many data sources, complete analysis, and efficient distribution of information. Whether you're performing economic dispatch, load planning and forecasting, condition-based maintenance, or just reviewing email, the method in which the data is delivered is important. Every hour in the work day is contentious, riddled with information overload. Information that is complete and uncluttered allows users to make more efficient decisions. That is certainly true in the real time world. The more specific and pertinent information is, the more valuable it is to the decision making process.

The past decade has marked one of the most exciting times in technology history. As the world becomes more connected than ever using the Internet, consumers and most certainly leading edge businesses have a multitude of methods to consume information. While news agencies worldwide offer services such as SMS messaging and websites tailored to mobile users to keep them up to date in real time about global events, some companies continue to face the challenge of operating in that same global real time environment. The SMS message or mobile web story is powerful because they're easy to access, they provide the most important information, and they can reach you anywhere you can get on the Internet or find a cell phone signal. Where were you when the last major world event happened? It likely didn't matter because you take advantage of technologies that keep you informed and connected in real time. Can you say the same for your business operations? It's time for Real Time.

Chapter Notes and References

Chapter 1—Cutlip definition from *Effective Public Relations*, 9th edition, Cutlip, Center and Broom, Pearson, New Jersey p. 1.

Chapter 8—As published in *Masonry Magazine*, Lionheart Publishing.

Chapter 10—As published in Bacon's Media Map online newsletter, *ExpertPR*.

Chapter 11—As published in *Masonry Magazine*, Lionheart Publishing.

Chapter 12—As published in Bacon's Media Map online newsletter, *ExpertPR*.

Chapter 14—This chapter was contributed by Sue MacDonald, Senior Analyst, Nielsen Buzzmetrics.

Chapter 19—As published in *Masonry Magazine*, Lionheart Publishing.

Chapter 20—As published in *Masonry Magazine*, Lionheart Publishing.

Chapter 23—As published in *Masonry Magazine*, Lionheart Publishing.

Chapter 24—The measurement section was contributed by Katie Paine, KDPaine & Partners.

Chapter 25—

- 1. Marianne Moody Jennings, *Business: Its Legal, Ethical and Global Environment* (2000), p. 573.
- 2. Marianne Moody Jennings, pp. 49-51 and *Making Ethical Decisions*, Josephson Institute of Ethics, www.josephsoninstitute.org (September 2004).
- 3. Gwendolyne Parks, class handout, October 2001 (1999).

Index

About the Author

Linda VandeVrede has nearly 25 years of experience helping companies of all sizes and at all stages enhance their market leadership position through proven public relations strategies. She has a Master's Degree in Mass Communications from Boston University, and a Bachelor's Degree in English from Dickinson College.

Linda has won the American Society of Business Publication Editors' Gold and Silver Awards for excellence in business writing, and is a member of the PRSA Counselor's Academy and the Arizona Technology Council. A frequent speaker for associations throughout the United States, she lives with her husband, Dale, in Scottsdale, Arizona.

For more information, please contact:

Website: www.vandevrede-pr.com
Phone: 480-551-1258
Email: linda@vandevrede-pr.com